ANNA SCHÄFFER
An example for the sick, the suffering and the poor

SCHNELL + STEINER

Anna Schäffer

AN EXAMPLE FOR THE SICK, THE SUFFERING AND THE POOR

Dedicated to
His Holiness
POPE BENEDICT XVI

GLORY BE TO THE FATHER
AND TO THE SON
AND TO THE HOLY SPIRIT,
AS IT WAS IN THE BEGINNING, IS NOW
AND WILL BE FOREVER. AMEN

With ecclesiastical permission
Prelate M. Fuchs, Vicar General
Regensburg, 29.02.2012

The author of this brief biography,
Mons. Georg Franz X. Schwager,
is Director of the Department for Beatification and Canonisation Processes
for the Diocese of Regensburg.

Bibliographic information published by the Deutsche Nationalbibliothek
The Deutsche Nationalbibliothek lists this publication in the Deutsche Nationalbibliografie;
detailed bibliographic data are available on the Internet at http://dnb.dnb.de .

2. Edition 2017
© 2017 Verlag Schnell & Steiner GmbH,
Leibnizstr. 13, D-93055 Regensburg
Translation: Sr. Nancy Celaschi, OSF
Printing: Grafisches Centrum Cuno GmbH & Co. KG, Calbe
Layout and graphics: Barbara Stefan, Regensburg
Cover Design: Barbara Stefan, Regensburg

ISBN 978-3-7954-2631-6

All rights reserved. Electronic or photomechanical reproduction of this book or excerpts thereof is prohibited
without the express permission of the publisher and the Diocesan Consistory of Regensburg.

Additional information about the publisher can be found at
www.schnell-und-steiner.de

Table of Contents

Childhood – Youth – Accident	8
Mission of Suffering – Seeking God and His Will in Suffering	17
Eucharistic Life – Source of Strength	23
Love for the Blessed Mother and the Rosary	28
The Grace of Heavenly Consolations	30
Apostolate of the Sickbed	35
Special Attention of Children, Young People and the Villagers	40
Her Last Years, Blessed Death and Fulfilment in God	43
Appreciation for and the Meaning of Anna Schäffer's Life's Work	48
Concluding Observations	56
Anna Schäffer's Poems	58
Excerpts from Anna Schäffer's Letters	65
Excerpts from Anna Schäffer's "Thoughts And Memories Of My Life Of Illness And My Longing For The Eternal Homeland"	67
Significant dates in the life of Anna Schäffer	68
Bibliography / References	69
Abbreviations	70
Portrait of Anna-Schäffer – Significance	70

Anna Schäffer from Mindelstetten (1882–1925). (Photographic archives; Photo: Horoba)

AN EXAMPLE FOR THE SICK, THE SUFFERING AND THE POOR

In Anna Schäffer from Mindelstetten we find a person who, despite dreadful physical suffering caused by a tragic accident and combined with extreme poverty, led a life of deep love of God and neighbour. The secret of her earthly existence was an interior union with Christ, a union which she did not lose despite sickness and suffering; however, it was precisely in and through the adverse circumstances of her life that, by the grace of God, she was able to deepen it more and more.

"In suffering and unpleasantness I gaze upon the cross,– and at the tabernacle! Praised be the Cross. – Praised be Jesus in the Holy Eucharist..!"[1]

This quote from one of Anna Schäffer's letters sums up what shaped the life of this simple maiden and from what she drew her strength. Here she reveals a decisive inclination to two of the supporting pillars of Catholic piety, which she learned in her childhood. Anna Schäffer grasped and gratefully accepted the cross and tabernacle as her daily claim, but equally so as a sign and means of God's grace.

---

[1] Anna Schäffer, Letter of 28.11.1922, in: BKR Abt. C.A.S. Proc. sup. perqu. Scriptorum D. 131–183 K. 12. The German expression, "Es lebe" is best rendered as Viva in Romance languages and/or "Hooray", "Hoorah", "Three cheers for " or "Long live.. " in English. None of these seem appropriate, so here and elsewhere in this translation it is rendered as "Praised be".

Childhood – Youth – Accident

Anna Schäffer was born on 18 February 1882, the daughter of a carpenter in the village of Mindelstetten, between Ingolstadt and Regensburg. Although the family was of modest means, Anna grew into a healthy, strong maiden. From her childhood she demonstrated a calm nature; piety and love of God were instilled in her through the Christian upbringing given her by her mother, Theres Schäffer (née Forster). After the death of her husband, the mother and her children tried to maintain the carpenter's shop "in poverty"[2]. Yet it was she who stood by Anna throughout the years of her illness and cared for her with great self-sacrifice.

Anna Schäffer at the age of nine.
(Photographic archives)

Anna Schäffer was no different than the other children of the village. "At school she studied, she was quick and neat about her work. She grew into a strong, well-raised girl, according to those who knew her at the time"[3]. A photograph taken during the May Festival in Ingolstadt, a well-known folk festival, shows the 16-year-old in this way. The most remarkable thing about her childhood and youth is that on the day of her First Communion, 12 April 1893, she dedicated herself to Jesus as an offering for sin. She did so in the following words, which we have written in Anna's own hand:

"Resolution at my First Holy Communion! Oh dear, good Jesus, today at my First Holy Communion I consecrate and offer to You my heart and soul. Do not leave me, O dear Jesus in this pilgrimage and do with me whatever You will; I also want always to be good and follow You, so that I can give you much joy. I want to atone for sins, oh dear Abba of Jesus. And if You will, oh good Abba, let me be an offering for sin; for all the dishonour and offenses committed against You, O good Jesus [...]. I commend to you as well, my dear parents and siblings, especially those difficult circumstances [...]. I commend to you as well my confessor, all my friends and enemies. I want to be good and follow you. Written on 12 April 1893. Renewed in the year 1914!"[4]

---
2 Cf. Rev. Carl Rieger, Report on Anna Schäffer of 4 February 1929, in: BKR Abt. C.A.S. Acts 1926–1930 K. 20.
3 Georg Schwaiger, Anna Schäffer von Mindelstetten. Ein Leben in der Gnade Gottes, Regensburg, 4th edition 2000, p. 4.
4 Quoted from: Emmeram H. Ritter, Anna Schäffer. Eine Selige aus Bayern, Regensburg 2012, p. 32.

Anna Schäffer at the May Festival in Ingolstadt. *(Photographic archives)*

Anna's request to be an oblation for sin to atone for offenses against God was heard and would ultimately become the decisive reality of her life.

Since she had harboured the wish to become a religious in a missionary Order, at the end of her formal schooling Anna tried to earn the necessary dowry by working in Regensburg and Landshut. Her sister Katharina reports that Anna helped care for the patients of a homeopathic doctor in Regensburg, especially those suffering from dermatological problems. Conditions there were "quite strict"[5]. Her own brother, who was an apprentice in Regensburg, was not allowed to visit her even once. However, to Anna's consolation in the garden of the place where she worked there was a chapel and she was able to go at five o'clock each morning to participate in the Mass. After the death of her father in January 1896, in accordance with her mother's wishes Anna left her job in Regensburg and went to work for some time on a farm. Then through the mediation of her parish priest, Father Carl Rieger (1862–1934), she came to Landshut[6]. There in a "dream" she would have the first indication of her life of suffering. Anna Schäffer reported this dream in one of her notebooks:

"Dream of June 1898

In June 1898 I had a very strange dream; obviously I call it a dream because I cannot think of any other way to describe it! I had not yet gone to bed, and the moon was shining brightly into my room! I said my night prayers and it was ten o'clock. When I was almost ready for bed, it suddenly became very dark around me and I was very afraid. Suddenly it became very bright and in front of me there was a figure standing; it was clothed with a blue robe and a red mantle, exactly like the apostles were dressed, or how I have often seen depictions of Jesus, the Good Shepherd! He also had a rosary in his hand; he spoke to me about the rosary and that I was not yet 20 years old, but that I would have to suffer very, very much. The figure also said that I would have to suffer for a very long time, even telling me the number of years, but I did not remember them, because as soon as the figure disappeared, I was so overcome with trembling and fear that I could no longer remember everything the figure had said. Then it became bright again, and the moon shone its gentle beams all night long in my room. I could hardly sleep the whole night long, because that face was always in my mind! I was 16 years old at the time, and two years later, at the age of 18, I had an accident; I was not yet 20 years old, and I already had to endure great sufferings, just as that figure had said. The face in my dreams is as clear in my mind as if it were only yesterday! Many times during my school years I dreamt of the dear Mother of God!"[7]

---

5 Report on the life of Anna Schäffer by her sister, Katharina Veit, née Schäffer, in: BKR Abt. C.A.S. Transcriptions: Thoughts and Memories/ Dream book/ Poetry/ Accounts concerning AS K. 16.
6 Cf. Rev. Carl Rieger, Report on Anna Schäffer of 4 February 1929, in: BKR Abt. C.A.S. Acts 1926–1930 K. 20.
7 BKR Abt. C.A.S. Proc. sup. perqu. Scriptorum D. I–XIII K.12a IV, S. 1–3 (quoted from the original).

In her biography of her sister, Katharina Veit explains that the morning after this dream experience Anna came home, but her mother wanted to send her back to her place of work in Landshut. Anna, however, quite shaken by the announcement of her suffering, was not about to be convinced[8].

Another important event in Anna Schäffer's life in the year 1898 was her personal consecration to the Blessed Virgin Mary. A short formula that is still extant gives us this information[9].

What was communicated to Anna Schäffer in her youthful dream in June 1898 would come to pass on 4 February 1901. While Anna was performing her household chores in the laundry of the forester's lodge in Stammham near Ingolstadt, where the head of the forest service, a Protestant, lived with his family[10], she suffered the tragic accident which would cause her great suffering until the day she died. The stovepipe over the water boiler had come loose from the wall, and Anna wanted to prevent any damage. In the process she slipped and both legs slid into the boiler filled with boiling lye above her knees. There are different accounts of the accident but we do not have Anna's personal memories of it. Therefore we must rely on the reports of outsiders. Her sister, Katharina Veit, describes the tragic events in the following manner:

"Anna fetched water from the well, and it was a very cold day, so her wet stockings and shoes froze on her. Anna wanted to thaw out her wooden shoes near the boiler. She leaned with one hand on the wall, and with the other hand she shoved the boiler better into the stovepipe. The wooden shoes thawed out and she slipped into the boiler, which was filled one third of the way with lye. She was scalded more by the steam than by the water."[11]

---

8 Cf. Report on the life of Anna Schäffer by her sister, Katharina Veit, née Schäffer, in: BKR Abt. C.A.S. Transcriptions: Thoughts and Memories/ Dream book/ Poetry/ Accounts concerning AS K. 16.
9 Cf. BKR Abt. C.A.S. Proc. sup. perqu. Scriptorum S. I–IV D. 1–43 K. 9.
10 Cf. Rev. Carl Rieger, Report on Anna Schäffer of 4 February 1929, in: BKR Abt. C.A.S. Acts 1926–1930 K. 20.
11 Cf. Report on the life of Anna Schäffer by her sister, Katharina Veit, née Schäffer, in: BKR Abt. C.A.S. Transcriptions: Thoughts and Memories/ Dream book/ Poetry/ Accounts concerning AS K. 16.

Former laundry of the Forester's lodge in Stammham, site of Anna's tragic accident on 4 February 1901, the results of which she suffered until her death. *(Photographic archives)*

The "Mission of Suffering" following the Crucified that God intended for Anna would now begin. Although it was bitterly cold that day, she was taken to the Hospital in Kösching and later given intensive treatment at a clinic in Erlangen. Her feet were healed, and Anna was able to walk somewhat and returned to work at the home of the forester's family who took her back[12]; however, her feet broke out again and eventually continued to fester until the end of her life[13]. Every four days Anna bound up her own festering wounds; only in the last three years of her life was this service compassionately performed by members of Father Rieger's nursing staff. The replacement of the bandages always caused her great pain. Anna's condition deteriorated so much that eventually it was impossible for her to leave her bed; she could only sit up, but she used that opportunity to read, knit and embroider[14], but most of all to engage in her letter-writing apostolate, which we will hear more about later.

---

12 Cf. Rev. Carl Rieger, Report on Anna Schäffer of 4 February 1929, in: BKR Abt. C.A.S. Acts 1926–1930 K. 20.
13 Cf. Rev. Carl Rieger, Letter of 5 February 1929, in: BKR Abt. C.A.S. Acts 1926–1930 K. 20.
14 Cf. Rev. Carl Rieger, Report on Anna Schäffer of 4 February 1929, in: BKR Abt. C.A.S. Acts 1926–1930 K. 20.

When her mother became very sick before the First World War and her health did not improve, many a visitor told Anna: *"You will be a great burden on society"*[15]. Anna bore the hurtful and unsettling comments with love. Indeed, through all these torments she maintained a great trust in divine Providence and assured all her visitors: *"[...] the dear Lord God will take care of everything"*[16].

Her great suffering was accompanied by material poverty. Anna and her mother had a disability pension of nine marks a month to live on. Through the generous contributions of people who were willing to help, they received their necessities[17]. Her operations were expensive, although the doctor showed great understanding. Father Rieger also supported the sick girl as well as he could. He had food brought to them and tried to arrange for a pension. At this time Anna and her mother were in an extremely dire state. Through handiwork and sewing, helped also by her sister, they tried to pay her medical costs in small payments[18]. Despite her own poverty Anna gladly practised works of charity, contributed to the missions, gave Mass offerings and made and donated a large Communion cloth to the parish church[19]. In order to keep peace in the family, she and her mother and sister left the family home and moved to other accommodations. The Forchhammer family took her in and gave her a lovely room in an agricultural estate not so far away and close to the parish church. Here Anna Schäffer remained, suffered and grew in holiness until her blessed passing. Anna's room was on the upper floor and her bed faced the parish church, enabling her to have a glimpse of the Tabernacle[20]. Here for the many years of her illness she awaited with longing the arrival of Father Rieger whenever he brought her Holy Communion.

We can imagine and understand the physical suffering Anna Schäffer endured as a result of her tragic accident from February 1901 until her death if we take time to study the report of her physician, Dr. Wäldin from Pförring. He describes Anna's situation and his medical care in detail:

"Anna Schäffer from Mindelstetten came to my medical studio on 3 May 1901 because of extensive burns on both lower legs. She received the burns from falling into a boiler with heated contents. Before coming to my studio the patient was in care and treatment for 90 days at the hospital in Köschin. Since at that time the support payments were finished, she was sent back to her mother's home.

---

15 Note by Anna Schäffer, dated 20 October 1918 – Continuation. : N° 2, quoted from the original text in: BKR Abt. C.A.S. Proc. sup. perqu. Scriptorum D. 1–43 K. 9.
16 Note by Anna Schäffer, dated 20 October 1918 – Continuation. : N° 2, quoted from the original text in: BKR Abt. C.A.S. Proc. sup. perqu. Scriptorum D. 1–43 K. 9.
17 Cf. Rev. Carl Rieger, Letter to Bishop Michael Buchberger of 5 October 1928, in: BKR Abt. C.A.S. Acts 1926–1930 K. 20.
18 Cf. Cf. Report on the life of Anna Schäffer by her sister, Katharina Veit, née Schäffer, in: BKR Abt. C.A.S. Transcriptions: Thoughts and Memories/ Dream book/ Poetry/ Accounts concerning AS K. 16.
19 Cf. Rev. Carl Rieger, Report vom 4. February 1929, in: BKR Abt. C.A.S. Acts 1926–1930 K. 20.
20 Cf. Report on the life of Anna Schäffer by her sister, Katharina Veit, née Schäffer, in: BKR Abt. C.A.S. Transcriptions: Thoughts and Memories/ Dream book/ Poetry/ Accounts concerning AS K. 16; also Rev. Carl Rieger, Letter of 5 February 1926, in: BKR Abt. C.A.S. Acts 1926–1930 K. 20.

My findings on first examining the patient were as follows: there was significant skin loss on both lower legs. They were covered with puffy, lightly bleeding growths, which constantly secreted runny pus.

The treatment was to be long-term. In repeated sessions the growths had to be shaved (sic!) in order to allow the wounds to dry out and to promote the healing of the wounds. Later skin transplants were applied, with some of her young women friends graciously consenting to serve as skin donors. The skin transplants were very successful but could not be continued because Anna Schäffer did not do well with anaesthesia, and without it the procedure was too painful. The treatment also was interrupted sometimes because Anna Schäffer was without means and she did not want to make a claim for public assistance nor did she want to make too many claims against her siblings, although she was generously supported by a sister and a brother. During my absence in the field I was able to visit and care for Anna Schäffer only on occasion during my periods of leave and during these war years as a result of her long confinement she developed paresis in both legs and clubfeet. The paresis was spastic, i.e., the muscles were constantly in a state of tension.

Because of this paresis Anna Schäffer's suffering was seriously worsened. Her wounds were, as mentioned already, not healed, and the patient refused any further operations because there did not seem to be a promise of the wounds closing. When the dressings were being changed, as in other situations, the muscle contraction in her legs induced contractions of the muscles throughout her body, so that the patient often lay for hours in seeming unconsciousness. The joyful disposition that she had previously exhibited diminished and morphine often had to be used to control the pain. Her food intake was very limited, so that one would have to wonder how the patient could live for so many years with such little nourishment.

On 5 October 1925 exhaustion freed Anna Schäffer from the painful suffering that she had endured for almost 25 years with an endless, most amazing patience." [21]

---

21 Original report of Dr. Wäldin, Pförring on 15 September 1931, in: BKR Abt. C.A.S. Acts 1931–1939 K. 21.

Anna Schäffer together with her mother, Theres Schäffer (1853–1928).   *(Photographic archives)*

Her spiritual director, who for many years was the eyewitness of her suffering, her parish priest, Father Carl Rieger, describes Anna's resignation to her fate in the following words in which he seeks to give a spiritual interpretation to her suffering:

"How the great sufferer rejoiced to be able to live in piety and innocence and for 25 years to accept the difficult trials of divine Providence and be able to bear them in suffering after the example of the Saviour! The pious one saw it as a loving call from the crucified Lord, her own task to gain an eternal reward. The deceased suffered with great patience. In the immeasurable suffering of 25 years I never heard an impatient word. Even in these last years, when she would cry out in pain, 'I cannot bear it any more', mention of the cross brought her peace, in her sleepless days and nights it gave her the strength to bear the further suffering that the Lord willed, to seek the Lord's will in compassion with Him, and in prayer to find the comfort and energy necessary for her sacrificial suffering, as long as God willed it. The deceased suffered with heroic faith. She offered her suffering for the whole Church, especially for the dying, and for all those who commended themselves to her; it was a joy for her to be an offering for souls" [22].

Parish Priest and Dean Carl Rieger (1862–1934), Anna Schäffer's loyal spiritual director for many years. *(Photographic archives)*

Father Rieger gives us a glimpse of those for whom Anna wanted to offer her suffering: for the Church, for the dying, and for all those who recommended themselves to her prayer. She wanted to suffer following Jesus Christ's example. She recognized this as her life's task. Looking at the cross and prayer gave her the strength to do it!

---

22 Remarks at the graveside of the virgin Anna Schäfer (sic!), who suffered and sacrificed for 25 years in Mindelstetten. Given on 8 October 1925 by Rev. Father Karl Rieger. Habbel Brothers' Press, Regensburg, in: BKR Abt. C.A.S. Acts 1921–1925 K. 19.

Mission of Suffering – Seeking God and His Will in Suffering

What Father Rieger said during Anna's funeral we find confirmed by her own words. Examples from her letters reveal to us her humble disposition and resignation towards her lot of suffering. She seeks to know God's plan and will for her and understands more and more her "mission of suffering". In a letter to her friend, Rosa Imlauer, Anna Schäffer writes:

"And we must always have our heart on the cross, – and the cross in our heart! Then we can always bear everything with love and joy, whatever crosses and sacrifices divine Providence sends us. [...] I often thank the dear God for giving me the ability to thank and maintaining it, so that I can thank Him for all the graces and suffering, etc. I want my every breath to be a prayer of thanksgiving and love" [23].

In another letter she admits:

"Most of all, I want to pray and suffer for the holy Church and her pastors. Each time at Holy Communion I ask the dear Saviour to preserve his Church and her pastors and send me instead the most horrible of martyrdoms and accept me as his little expiatory sacrifice" [24].

Anna Schäffer learned to praise God in everything, to thank Him and to try to fulfil God's will. This is clearly seen from a few citations from her countless letters:

"My whole body is always burdened with pain, from the sole of my feet, to the crown of my head. My hands too hurt so much. My God, I thank you for every hour of suffering! My God, I love You! In total surrender, oh my God, I have given myself to You as a sacrifice; – let me suffer according to Your pleasure; – let me suffer on the cross on which you have placed me – until I am acceptable to you. With love and willingness I take up the chalice of bitterness and thank You until my last breath. Your holy will, oh my God, is enough for me in everything and I want to die completely to my own will. This union with God's holy will allows me to recognize in everything that suffering is my training for heaven." [25]

"I no longer thirst for earthly comfort, but for bitterness and pain that I can bear for Your honour." [26]

---

23 Anna Schäffer, Letter of 17 December 1921, in: BKR Abt. C.A.S. Proc. sup. perqu. Scriptorum D. 77–130 K. 11 (quoted from the original).
24 Anna Schäffer, Letter of 29 January 1919, in: BKR Abt. C.A.S. Proc. sup. perqu. Scriptorum D. 44–76 K. 10 (quoted from the original).
25 Anna Schäffer, Letter of 7 September 1921, in: BKR Abt. C.A.S. Proc. sup. perqu. Scriptorum D. 77–130 K. 11 quoted from the original).
26 Anna Schäffer, Letter of 28 December 1921, in: BKR Abt. C.A.S. Proc. sup. perqu. Scriptorum D. 77–130 K. 11 (quoted from the original).

"And with holy love and joy I want to embrace and kiss my little cross and, according to God's will, suffer until I am ready for eternal love, for eternal life. Oh my God, I praise You more for all the sufferings that You give me than for all the unending joys I have received from you. One does not achieve true divine love without having drunk from the chalice of suffering, – without experiencing the absence of light – and suffering abandonment by God. In the school of the cross all the lessons include self-mastery and abnegation of one's own will. Everything, everything praise and bless the Lord, I would like to cry out with the three young men in the fiery furnace. In God's holy will and praising God I want to spend every moment of my life and suffering. My God, I thank You! My God, I love You!" [27]

With great generosity Anna comes to the decision to offer her life and suffering to God in expiation for the conversion of sinners. In this sense she sees her life as a "little martyrdom". She shares this insight with her friend Anna Bortenhauser:

"After my death, you may think, dear Anna, that my life was a little martyrdom and that I may never express in word or writing how much I had to suffer. And with every new day I thirst for new sufferings and for souls for their conversion and salvation" [28].

Anna Schäffer places herself securely in God's holy will. Thus she recognizes her suffering more and more as a grace, not something that she must suffer, but that she "may" suffer. She testifies to this in a letter from the last years of her life:

"[...] There is not even 15 minutes in which I do not suffer. My suffering has lasted for more than 21 years. Daily I experience to some degree the nails of the cross and the points of the crown of thorns. Yet I am so happy and thank the dear Saviour for everything that I have already had to suffer. After such a long and difficult suffering, it is the Lord's will that by His grace I am still living; – I live on the cross and I also hope to end it happily through and with the cross. In God's holy will and praising God I want to spend every moment of my life and suffering. And how happy I shall be, when the number of my days of suffering has come to an end, to go to Jesus forever." [29]

---

27 Anna Schäffer, Letter of 4 April 1922, in: BKR Abt. C.A.S. Proc. sup. perqu. Scriptorum D. 131–183 K. 12 (quoted from the original).
28 Anna Schäffer, Letter of 7 February 1920, in: BKR Abt. C.A.S. Proc. sup. perqu. Scriptorum D. 77–130 K. 11 (quoted from the original).
29 Anna Schäffer, Letter of 17 March 1922, in: BKR Abt. C.A.S. Proc. sup. perqu. Scriptorum D. 131–183 K. 12 (quoted from the original).

The window marked with the cross indicates Anna Schäffer's room, in which she sanctified herself and to a heroic degree offered her suffering for the conversion of sinners. (Photo: Böckler)

Her sickbed became her "work place of suffering"[30] and in recalling her youthful desire to become a religious and consecrate her life to God, a convent cell as well:
"I tell myself: My bed is God's will! And whatever I have to suffer in this condition I gladly accept with joy and thus I hope that God's will and my suffering are one [...]. My God, I thank You! My God, I love You!"[31]
"Whenever I see such a lovely soul go to the convent, it awakens my great longing for that holy, sacrificial vocation which I had begun to forge in my own plans. And if I no longer have the physical health to go to the convent, I shall lead an even more intense spiritual life and see my sickbed as a quiet cell in which I can also observe the three holy religious vows"[32].

After her tragic accident in February 1901 her life's task was to seek and find God in sickness and pain; indeed, from the suffering of Jesus she wants to learn to understand and see her own suffering. Therein she should find her fulfilment.
"We want to learn suffering from the suffering Saviour and in holy simplicity and willingness we want to follow in the footsteps of his way of the cross, because we cannot possibly understand our own suffering if we have not learned to observe and understand Jesus' suffering. Because suffering in body and soul gives us an opportunity to learn to understand so much and be able to experience how greatly the divine crucified one suffered so many types of suffering... and He did it all out of love for us poor sinners!"[33]

In the hard school of suffering Anna learned to recognise God's will and always accept it joyfully. She understood infirmity and poverty as a loving call from the crucified, to resemble Him in this way. She did not understand poverty only as material poverty, but also as the experience of spiritual poverty, an inner desolation and emptiness, human weakness. In this context she affords us a deep and precious glimpse into her inner life.
"Do you not know that the edelweiss blooms – where all the other flowers no longer bloom, – on the heights of the Alps? [...] To it I also compare all the pious, God-loving souls, – whose only concern is to strive to climb upward on the path of virtue. And just like the edelweiss they continue to bloom joyfully in spiritual aridity – cold – and dryness to the praise and glory of their Creator on the heights of the mountains of perfection. [...] How good would it be if we could always experience tangible spiritual consolation? And how much more would the life of grace of our soul be in danger of standing still rather than going forward? And are not wind

---

30 Anna Schäffer, Letter of 24 December 1916, in: BKR Abt. C.A.S. Proc. sup. perqu. Scriptorum S. I–IV D. 1–43 K. 9.
31 Anna Schäffer, Letter of 17 March 1922, in: BKR Abt. C.A.S. Proc. sup. perqu. Scriptorum D. 131–183 K. 12 (quoted from the original).
32 Anna Schäffer, Letter of 21 September 1921, in: BKR Abt. C.A.S. Proc. sup. perqu. Scriptorum D. 77–130 K. 11 (quoted from the original).
33 Anna Schäffer, Letter of 13 August 1919, in: BKR Abt. C.A.S. Proc. sup. perqu. Scriptorum D. 44–76 K. 10 (quoted from the original).

and rain a part of the process of fruit-bearing and ripening? Just as well in the spiritual life we cannot arrive at the mature fruit, if we did not have to bear – spiritual aridity,– cold, dryness, abandonment"[34].

"In the valley of humility and self denial grow and thrive the most beautiful flowers which the heavenly Gardener loves so much. [...] We learn each day to recognise our weakness and wretchedness more and more"[35].

The sense in which Anna Schäffer accepted her "mission of suffering" and also counselled others to accept it is revealed most of all in her "spiritual prescription":
"If you want to enjoy health of spirit, take a root of faith, some green leaves of hope, some roses of love; frankincense of repentance; myrrh of mortification, some wood of the cross; bind all of these together in a bundle of resignation to God's holy will, place it in the vessel of silent prayer and baste it with the wine of holy cheerfulness and with the water of holy moderation and place the vessel on the fire of divine love; cook it all together and then place it in the cool garden of meditation and cover it with the lid of holy silence. And if you take a cup of this precious drink early each morning and late each evening, you will achieve spiritual health, which is my wish and prayer for you. Given as such in the pharmacy of the love-filled wound in the side of our Lord Jesus Christ. My Jesus mercy!"[36]

With this disposition Anna Schäffer bore not only physical suffering. In the same manner she bore the pain of her brother's accounts about her in the pub. Jealous people are always willing to listen to that kind of gossip. Anna bore the suspicions and even the harsh attacks of the evil one, as she often told her mother, which she overcame by sprinkling herself with holy water[37]. On the day of Christ's passion and on "worldly sin days"[38] she usually had to bear greater pain than on other days.

---

34 Anna Schäffer, Letter of 16 March 1920, in: BKR Abt. C.A.S. Proc. sup. perqu. Scriptorum D. 77–130 K. 11 quoted from the original).
35 Anna Schäffer, Letter of 17 November 1920, in: BKR Abt. C.A.S. Proc. sup. perqu. Scriptorum D. 77–130 K. 11 (quoted from the original).
36 Note by Anna Schäffer in: BKR Abt. C.A.S. Proc. sup. perqu. Scriptorum D. I–XIII K. 12a, A III, S. 105.
37 Cf. Rev. Carl Rieger, Report of 4 February 1929, in: BKR Abt. C.A.S. Acts 1926–1930 K. 20; Cf. also Report on the life of Anna Schäffer by her sister, Katharina Veit, née Schäffer, in: BKR Abt. C.A.S. Transcriptions: Thoughts and Memories/ Dream book/ Poetry/ Accounts concerning AS K. 16,
38 Cf. Rev. Carl Rieger, Letter of 5 February 1926, in: BKR Abt. C.A.S. Acts 1926–1930 K. 20.

Anna Schäffer. *(Oil painting by Prechtl 1999; Photo: Horoba)*

Eucharistic Life – Source of Strength

In the face of the adverse circumstances of Anna Schäffer's life, the question invariably arises: What, or much more, WHO gave her the strength to bear her suffering and pain, her increasing infirmity, her poverty? She herself offers the answer towards the end of her life. In an undated letter to her friend Lina she admits:

"My greatest strength is Holy Communion!" [39]

No one can understand Anna Schäffer's life and personality without understanding her great love for Jesus Christ in Communion, in the Sacrament of the Holy Eucharist. Father Rieger, her conscientious parish priest, visited Anna daily, as much as he could, in order to bring her Holy Communion. [40] He knew how much she relied on the divine strength she received from her Eucharistic Lord. She feels a bond of gratitude to the parish priest for his loyal service.

"Oh how thankful I am to You, O dearest Saviour, that in all my cross and suffering you have given me such a generous guide and comfort in our esteemed parish priest." [41]

In the reception of Holy Communion and in loving immersion in the mystery of the abiding presence of the Lord in the Blessed Sacrament Anna finds the necessary strength and comfort not to be overwhelmed by her suffering. Strengthened by the Sacrament of the Eucharist, which she calls her "sunny source of grace", she feels so happy that, in spite of her suffering, she would never want to exchange places with a "worldly princess". She writes:

"As for the rest, my condition is always under the shadow of the cross and suffering; – but also in the clear sunny source of grace of the Most Holy Sacrament – here suffering and joy are mixed together; at this source of grace my suffering becomes joy and that is my quiet resting place at every hour of the day!" [42]

"I cannot begin to express in writing how happy I am each time after Holy Communion. Oh, then I forget all my suffering in this life and the longing of my poor soul draws me at each moment to pray to my hidden God and Saviour in the Most Holy Sacrament! Indeed [...] in those holy hours I am often so happy that for all the world I would not exchange my bed of suffering with any worldly princess" [43].

---

39 "The last letter of Anna Schäffer taken from the original", in: BKR Abt. C.A.S. Proc. sup. perqu. Scriptorum D. 131–183 K. 12.
40 Cf. Rev. Carl Rieger, Letter of 5 February 1926, in: BKR Abt. C.A.S. Acts 1926–1930 K. 20.
41 Anna Schäffer, Composition of 20 October 1918, in: BKR Abt. C.A.S. Proc. sup. perqu. Scriptorum S. I–IV D. 1–43 K. 9 (quoted from the original).
42 Anna Schäffer, Letter of 29 January 1919, in: BKR Abt. C.A.S. Proc. sup. perqu. Scriptorum D. 44–76 K. 10 (quoted from the original).
43 Anna Schäffer, Letter of 30 December 1917, in: BKR Abt. C.A.S. Proc. sup. perqu. Scriptorum S. I–IV D. 1–43 K. 9 (quoted from the original).

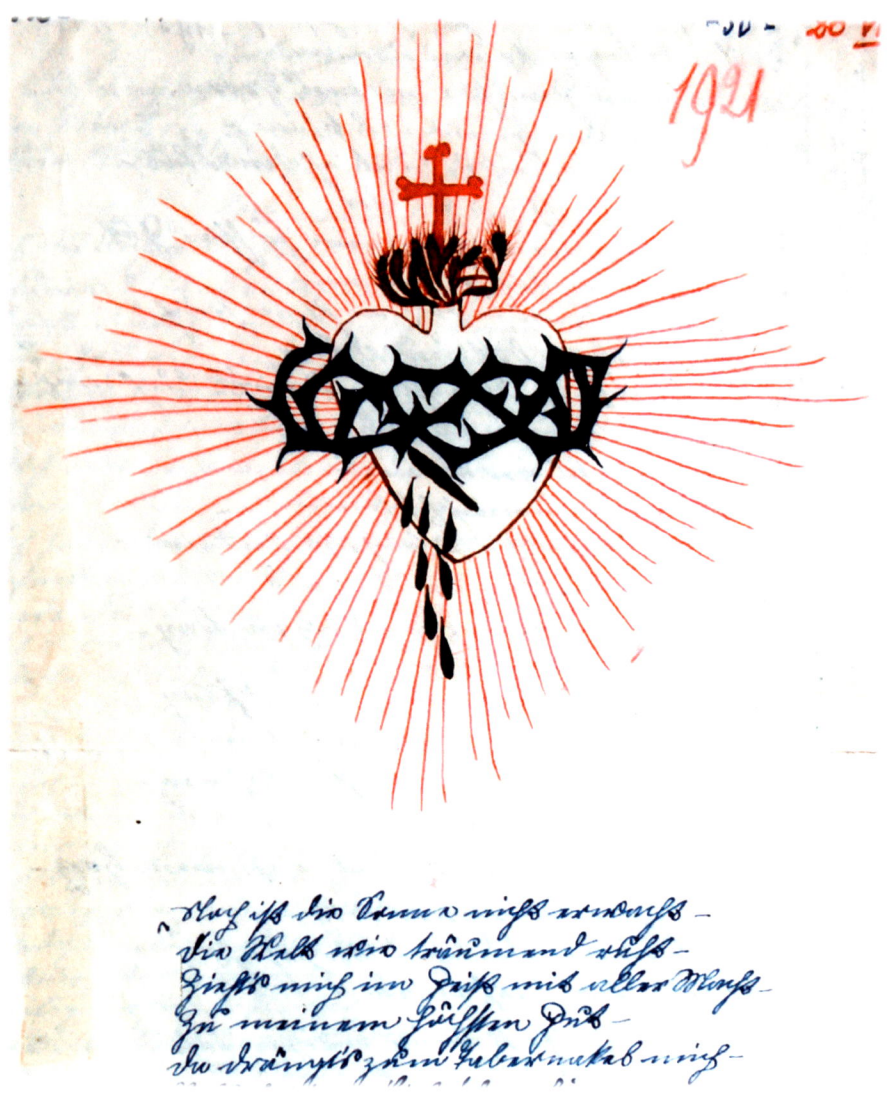

The Most Sacred Heart of Jesus as depicted in a letter by Anna Schäffer on 20 July 1921. It was chosen as her logo. The flames from the Heart are composed of ears of wheat, a reference to the Sacrament of the Eucharist in which we encounter the expiatory love of Jesus. (Photographic archives)

"In holy prayer and in Holy Communion we find our greatest consolation on the sickbed. And how happy are the hours after Holy Communion, when the Lord of heaven and earth dwells in our poor heart. Oh how happily we then shout: 'Let me rest on Your Heart – That loves me so sweetly – Lighter will become the pains– that seemed so heavy and hard to me!'" [44]

Her deep longing for the Eucharistic Lord also leads Anna to express herself in verse, which she often included in the beginning of her letters. Two examples are given here, while others can be found in the appendix.

A little church nearby

*"How lovely it is to live –
With a little church nearby
With our dear God as a neighbour
What could possibly be better?
The flickering of the perpetual lamp
Is light during my night –
I sleep in peace and quiet –
The Saviour keeps watch for me.
My first glance in the morning
Falls upon the little church
I thank the Lord in the Sacrament
For his protection and my rest
And when the day brings me hours
Filled with pain –
Then I know I can always flee
To the heart of my Jesus.
A quarter of an hour each evening
To be all alone with Him
Contains a sea of bliss,
the whole of heaven –
O dear Saviour –
Hear my prayer–
Allow me, once I reach heaven
To be your neighbour there as well!"* [45]

---

[44] Anna Schäffer, Letter of 12 March 1917, in: BKR Abt. C.A.S. Proc. sup. perqu. Scriptorum D. I IV D. 1 43 K. 9 quoted from the original).In the original German this is a four-line poem of trochaic tetrameter with an ABAB rhyme scheme.
[45] Anna Schäffer, Letter of 22 November 1918, in: BKR Abt. C.A.S. Proc. sup. perqu. Scriptorum D. 44–76 K. 10 (quoted from the original).

Early morning, before first light

Early morning, before first light
A little silver bell will ring
And a shepherd in a white garment
Will bring me my Saviour!

Early morning, before first light
My room becomes bright and shining
Holy angels will kneel down
Waiting silently at the threshold!

Early morning, before first light
Trembling will I say three times
Jesus Christ, I am not worthy
To bear you in my breast!

Early morning, before first light
Turning to me the Lord says,
Not to the strong but to the weak
Has my Father sent me!

Early morning, before first light
I bear him in the depths of my heart
And forget my life,
My pain and suffering for an hour!

When the first light doth appear
He has quietly left me
However, in my little cell
Wonderful fragrances linger!

A crimson red rose,
He left me on his departure
Saying, during the course of the hours
Do not let your brightness fade!

Think of me and abide in my love
Unite with me in pain and suffering.
Behold, I come and I come again
Early morning, before first light!" [46]

---

[46] Anna Schäffer, Letter of 29 June 1917, in: BKR Abt. C.A.S. Proc. sup. perqu. Scriptorum S. I–IV D. 1–43 K. 9 (quoted from the original).

The Blessed Sacrament of the Eucharist, symbolised by a chalice and host, surrounded by thorns and roses, on the cover page of a letter from Anna to Anna Bortenhauser, 6 September 1918.
(Photo: Horoba)

A still extant notebook with entries from the years 1918 to 1923 witnesses to Anna Schäffer's gratitude for the great gift of the Eucharist. In it she kept count of the number of times she received Communion.[47] And in his eulogy Father Rieger, who through his visits to her sickbed obtained like no other an insight into her interior relationship with the Eucharistic Lord, summarised it in the following words:

"She could never attend Holy Mass in the Church, so in her sickroom she sought a place from which she could see the church, and from there she participated in the Eucharistic sacrifice, since in spirit she drew near to the Saviour in the Tabernacle; she took more nourishment from prayer than from food, and more serenity than earthly relief; in the first years of her suffering she counted her holy Communions and after the great privilege granted by Pius X with the greatest spiritual joy she daily received Holy Communion in her sickroom, even when due to weakness she could hardly say a longer prayer, even on the last days of her earthly suffering. With what purity of soul, with what faith-filled trust in the Saviour she gazed upon the Host, the Lord Himself knows as does her holy guardian angel, and both the priest who would bring Holy Communion to her sickroom, and those who were nearby were also able to note the renewed energy she received to bear her sufferings." [48]

---

47 Cf. BKR Abt. C.A.S. Proc. sup. perqu. Scriptorum D. 131–183 K. 12.
48 Remarks at the graveside of the virgin Anna Schäfer (sic!), who suffered and sacrificed for 25 years in Mindelstetten. Given on 8 October 1925 by Rev. Father Karl Rieger. Habbel Brothers' Press, Regensburg, in: BKR Abt. C.A.S. Acts 1921–1925 K. 19.

Love for the Blessed Mother and the Rosary

Anna Schäffer's life and suffering were supported and encompassed by prayer, most of all by a meditative abiding in God's presence, which praying the rosary allowed her to do. Her rosary accompanied her day and night; she referred to it affectionately as her "game of roses":

"And then too there is the holy rosary which I so much love to pray; by praying the rosary one can obtain so much from our dear Saviour...! I have my rosary beads as my faithful companion the whole night long in my hands which are often burning with the fire of my illness and by day it is my "game of roses" (as I often call it) whenever I am not knitting, writing, or doing anything else" [49].

Anna Schäffer's Rosary. (Photo: Feldmann)

In addition to her youthful consecration to Mary, she remained true to the Mother of God her whole life long. *"Mary my Mother, – lead me to Jesus ....!"* [50], thus she still expressed her wish and prayer in the last years of her life. She especially entrusted herself to the Mother of Sorrows, asking her to help her to love the cross and suffering, as Mary herself did [51].

In an undated writing we have the following prayer of Anna Schäffer to Mary:

"Holy Mother of Sorrows, lead us to Calvary! May your pain – your hatred of sin – – become our own! Teach us to recognise the cross! –...–. .. mortal agony ... the love of Jesus .... and our ingratitude...! and give us always a burning thirst to work for the salvation of immortal souls, – to pray and suffer for them, and that we may always spend our days in the love of the Eucharistic Heart of Jesus in the Blessed Sacrament." [52]

---

49 Anna Schäffer, Letter of 16 February 1922, in: BKR Abt. C.A.S. Proc. sup. perqu. Scriptorum D. 131–183 K. 12 (quoted from the original).
50 Anna Schäffer, Letter of 28 February 1923, in: BKR Abt. C.A.S. Proc. sup. perqu. Scriptorum D. 131–183 K. 12 (quoted from the original).
51 Cf. Anna Schäffer, Letter of 21 September 1917, in: BKR Abt. C.A.S. Proc. sup. perqu. Scriptorum S. I–IV D. 1–43 K. 9.
52 Undated notation of Anna Schäffer, in: BKR Abt. C.A.S. Proc. sup. perqu. Scriptorum D. 131–183 K. 12 (quoted from the original).

In a poem she expresses her childlike love for the Mother of God and her hope to be able to see Mary's face in eternity:

> "Blessed is he who in springtime
> Already knows your sweet name
> From the beginning of life to the tomb
> Filially calls you his mother.
> One day the Angel of Death will call,
> But he will not call him with the scythe
> He will call him with the lily stalk
> To gaze on Mary's face." [53]

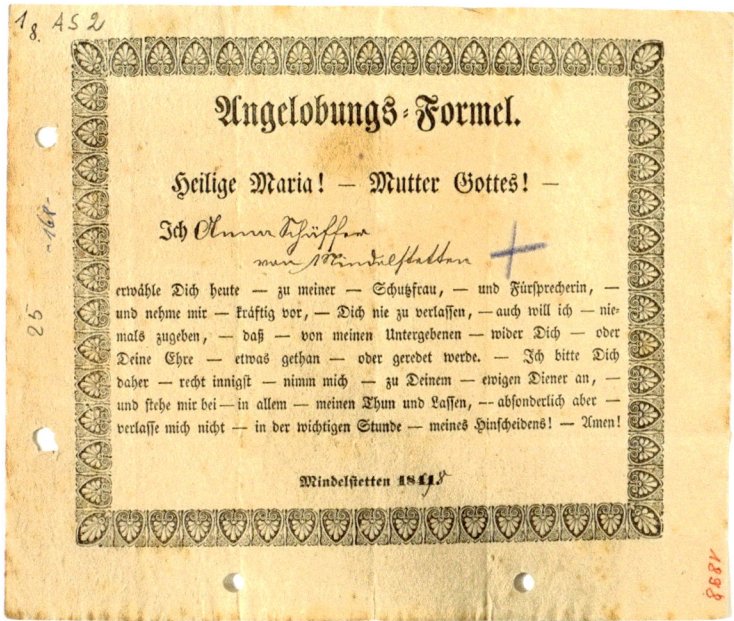

Formula by which in 1898 Anna Schäffer consecrated herself to the Blessed Virgin Mary.
(Photo: Horoba)

---

53 Undated notation of Anna Schäffer in: BKR Abt. C.A.S. Proc. sup. perqu. Scriptorum D. 131–183 K. 12 (quoted from the original).

The Grace of Heavenly Consolations

In addition to her vocation to suffering, God also gifted Anna Schäffer with special graces and heavenly consolations that led Father Rieger to recommend to her a special way of thanking the Lord[54]. Bishop Rudolf Graber (1962-1982) summarised Anna Schäffers suffering and extraordinary graces in his homily for the 50th anniversary of her death in the following words:
"The goal of her [Anna Schäffer's] life was horribly altered; however, she grew ever deeper in the mystery of the cross [...]. One must not think that everything came easily to her. She confessed that sometimes things were very difficult for her when her wounds were being dressed. However, the thought that she had offered herself entirely to God gave her the strength to endure the greatest of pain. Anna Schäffer entered like few other souls into the mystery of the cross. She fulfilled the "with" of the Apostle Paul to the utmost degree, to be crucified with Christ (Rom 6:6), and to be sure – and this is the real secret – in the same attitude with Christ, who gave himself as a ransom for all (1 Tim 2:6). [...]. For the sake of truthfulness, however, we may not overlook one thing in the life of our Anna Schäffer. Her 25 years of physical suffering were also lightened through the interior joy that was given to her from her mysterious contacts with the Saviour, the Mother of God, the angels and the saints: 'United with Jesus I am happy at all times. And although my physical pain is great, in my heart I feel a blessedness that I can never express.' Exterior suffering and interior joy are balanced. How could it be otherwise? No human being could bear such pain and suffering for so long. Basically suffering itself is changed into deep, inner joy"[55].

Among these extraordinary signs and examples of grace we must count first of all her "dreams" which she recorded for her spiritual director without his knowledge[56]. In her letters too she reports on them. Thus she makes mention of her encounters with several persons who the Church has since beatified or canonised. Among them we can mention Gemma Galgani (1878-1903), Gabriel Possenti (1838-1862), Anna Maria Taigi (1769-1837) and even Thérèse of Lisieux (1873-1897).

---

54 Cf. Rev. Carl Rieger, Letter to Bishop. Michael Buchberger of 5 October 1928, in: BKR Abt. C.A.S. Acts 1926-1930 K. 20.
55 From a homily of Bishop Rudolf Graber († 1992) on the 50th anniversary of the death of Anna Schäffer, in: Die Feier des Stundengebetes. Eigenfeiern des Bistums Regensburg. Authentische Ausgabe für den liturgischen Gebrauch. Herausgegeben im Auftrag des Bischofs von Regensburg, Regensburg 2011, S. 41 f.; Cf. Die Botschaft von Mindelstetten. Homily at Mass for the 50th anniversary of the death of the Servant of God Anna Schäffer in the Parish Church in Mindelstetten – 26. July 1975, in: Stärke Deine Brüder. Predigten-Ansprachen-Vorträge von Bischof Dr. Dr. h. c. Rudolf Graber. Veröffentlicht vom Bischöflichen Domkapitel Regensburg als Ehrengabe zum 75. Geburtstag des Diözesanbischofs, Regensburg 1978, S. 75-79.
56 Cf. Rev. Carl Rieger, Letter of 5 February 1926, in: BKR Abt. C.A.S. Acts 1926-1930 K. 20.

In a letter of 7 March 1917 she gives a detailed report of her encounter with Thérèse in a dream to the religious Tatona from Pirmasens in the Palatinate:

Saint Thérèse of Lisieux (1873–1897).
(Photographic archives)

"I have a great love for Sister Thérèse of the Child Jesus (St. Thérèse of Lisieux) and honour her daily; I first learned about her in August of last year! Before that I had never even heard her name and on 13 August in a dream I saw standing by my bed a nun with a brown habit and a white mantle. And she consoled me in my suffering, and said that on a sickbed the virtue of courage is especially necessary. She was so friendly and loving and her face radiated such a light that the whole room was bright. Then I said to her in my dream, 'oh, dear Sister, stay with me here for a while' and she smiled and said: 'The time is short, I must now hurry over to the parish house.' Then she gave me her hand and left, and from my window I saw her going over to the parish house. Then I awoke and I thought to myself that I had never seen such a nun wearing that particular habit. Then I prepared myself for Holy Communion, and after Holy Communion, when Mass was already over, a young girl who had just visited the parish house came and brought me two holy pictures of Sister Thérèse of the Child Jesus. When I saw them I was frightened, and I said, indeed, this is the nun of whom I dreamt last night; she looked exactly like the one on the holy card: – Sister Thérèse, with her crucifix adorned with roses –: Since that time I have a great love for her and will never forget her as long as I am numbered among the living!" [57]

---

[57] Anna Schäffer, Letter of 7 March 1917, in: BKR Abt. C.A.S. Proc. sup. perqu. Scriptorum S. I–IV D. 1–43 K. 9 (quoted from the original).

An exceptional event marked Anna Schäffer's mystical stigmatization in October 1910. She described it in this way:

> "On 4 October 1910, the feast of St. Francis, I was making a Holy Hour during the night, as I do each day. (This and all my other devotions I pray in the spiritual presence of the Most Holy Sacrament.)[*Followed by a passage that is illegible] I had been praying for a while when suddenly I was surrounded by a wonderful light which penetrated my whole spirit and body and I saw the dear Saviour in this sea of light and He said to me: I have accepted you for sins against my most Holy Sacrament, and at Holy Communion from tomorrow onwards you shall feel those pains of my Passion whereby I have redeemed, by which I have spared your wretched self nothing. Suffer, offer and make atonement in quiet hiddenness. Then the dear Saviour disappeared. My whole body shook and I cried a lot over my many sins and I asked the dear Saviour to be gracious and merciful to me, a poor sinner. It was now one o'clock in the morning, and I could not sleep. I prepared myself for the Holy Communion which I was to receive that same morning. When in the morning the parish priest brought me Holy Communion and in front of the host I prayed the prayer: Domine non sum dignus ...., at the three prayers I saw five fiery rays emanate from the sacred Host, and like lightning they struck my hands, feet and side, and I immediately experienced an inexpressible pain in the above-mentioned members. When I had received Holy Communion, I felt such an interior fire that I thought I would burn up. My God, be merciful to me a poor sinner..! I have had to experience this suffering without interruption since 4 October 1910 and I always have such terrible pain on my forefeet, hands, heart and head. [...] O my dear Jesus, let me continue my hidden suffering, as long as it is Your holy will. [...] I ask for only one thing from the depths of my heart: Leave unto me and give me always Holy Communion. You, You alone ...! [...] Written on 20 October 1918."[58]

In order to avoid any sensationalism and go on suffering in secret, she asked the Lord to take away her visible wounds – which in her report on the stigmatisation she referred to as "bluish red spots ". She was prepared to bear more pain for this purpose. Her prayer was granted.

Father Rieger also testified to Anna Schäffer's relationship with her guardian angel as an extraordinary grace. "As surely as she revealed her sickness to me, so too she reported that she saw her guardian angel and he gave her comfort"[59].

---

58 Note of Anna Schäffer from 20 October 1918, in: BKR Abt. C.A.S. Proc. sup. perqu. Scriptorum D. 1–43 K. 9 (quoted from the original).
59 Rev. Carl Rieger, Report on Anna Schäffer of 4 February 1929 (copy), in: BKR Abt. C.A.S. Acts 1926–1930 K. 20.

Anna Schäffer's Stigmatisation.   (Oil painting by Josef Kneuttinger from 2005; Photo: Zacharias)

Portrait of Anna Schäffer. (Oil painting by Winfried Tonner in 1999; Photo: Rappl)

Apostolate of the Sickbed

Anna used her remaining time and energy on her sickbed for an extensive and admirable apostolate. She prepared a formal daily schedule, which she filled with meditation on spiritual reading and the daily activities that she was able to perform[60]. Filled with thoughts of reparation, she understood her suffering and all that she could do, despite her confinement to bed, as a ministry for others, like a "key", that would open heaven's gates.

"I have three keys to heaven", she writes. "The largest is made of raw iron and is heavy in weight: that is my suffering! The second is my needle....The third is my pen...! With all these keys I will work hard each day to open heaven's gate, and each key shall be embellished with three crosses and three crowns: prayer, penance and self-denial!"[61]

Cardinal Augustin Bea. S.J. (1881–1968) once remarked: "Suffering is the most effective apostolic method"[62]. Anna paraphrased this conviction graphically with her comment about the heaviest key to heaven. It was precisely this key of suffering that changed her life into a "Love Story"[63], in which she offered her suffering in union with Christ in reparation for the conversion of sinners, in order to open heaven's gates not only for herself, but for others as well. The second key, her "needle", describes her activity as a seamstress. Even on her sickbed Anna gladly did needlework and embroidery, in order to add a little income to her small pension,

Cloth embroidered by Anna Schäffer. (Photographic archives)

---

60 Cf. Rev. Carl Rieger, Report on Anna Schäffer of 4 February 1929, in: BKR Abt. C.A.S. Acts 1926–1930 K. 20.
61 Anna Schäffer, Thoughts and Memories of my Life of Sickness – and my Longing for the Heavenly Homeland!, in: BKR Abt. CAS K. 12a XII (quoted from the original).
62 Citation from: Alfons Maria Weigl, Geschichte einer Liebe, Altötting, 15th edition, 1998, S. 151.
63 Alfons Maria Weigl, Geschichte einer Liebe, Altötting, 15th edition, 1998, S. 151.

as was already mentioned. She performed this work, however, in order to give joy to others. To this day we have a few samples of her work, including cloths to be used in administering the Anointing of the Sick or Communion for the Sick. The greatest part of her remaining time and energy, however, she dedicated to an extensive letter-writing apostolate that reached far beyond her homeland, in order to offer comfort most of all the sick and those who found themselves in difficult situations in life. She also responded to their questions, their needs and distress. For her letter-writing apostolate Anna used a sort of writing desk on her sickbed[64]. She gladly kept in written contact with her friends, some of whom were able to pursue a religious vocation, and other acquaintances to whom she felt an obligation of gratitude. Thus her "pen" became her third key to heaven. Concerning her interior attitude to her letter-writing apostolate she noted:

"I always wrote what was in my heart; [...] what good would it do if I would write whole books and my poor soul was far removed from what I had written; and would not God's grace be the true possession of the heart and take effect in it? Remaining little in the eyes of all, oh, that is what makes one happy and brings us great interior peace"[65].

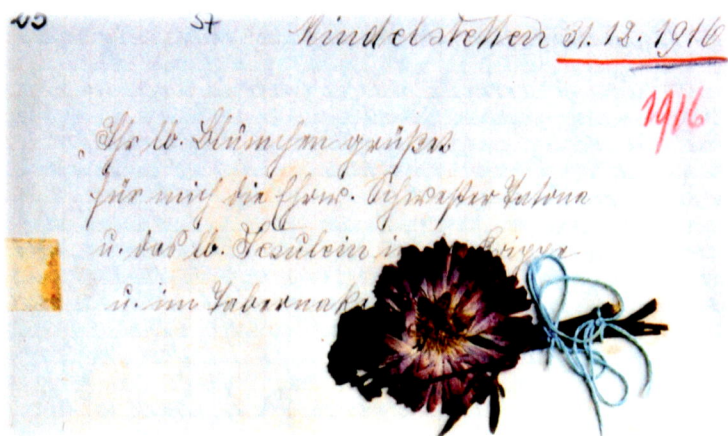

Anna Schäffer liked to decorate her letters with dried flowers.
(Photographic archives)

In her letters Anna Schäffer also shows a tendency towards poetry. Countless pieces of her writing begin with a long or short poem; many of them are also accompanied by lovely drawings of the Sacred Heart of Jesus, the cross or a Eucharistic chalice. Anna also liked to put dried flowers on her letters, some of

---

64 Cf. Rev. Carl Rieger, Report on Anna Schäffer of 4 February 1929, in: BKR Abt. C.A.S. Acts 1926–1930 K. 20.
65 Anna Schäffer, Letter of 1 September 1920, in: BKR Abt. C.A.S. Proc. sup. perqu. Scriptorum D. 77–130 K. 11 (quoted from the original).

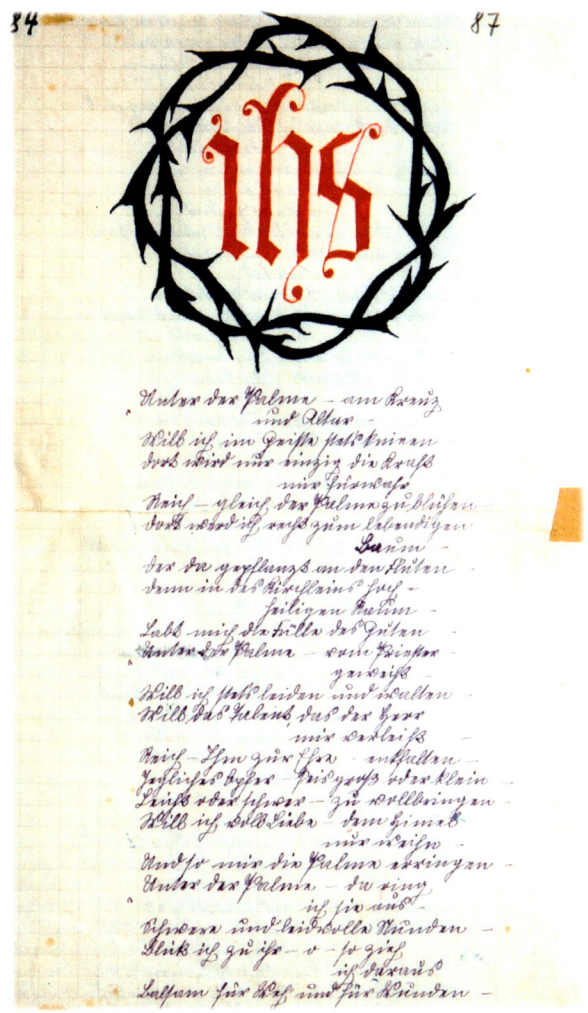

A typical drawing of Anna Schäffer on her letters.
(Photographic archives)

which are still extant. In her poetry Anna reflects her thoughts, most of them concerning her greatest requests: esteem and honour for the Most Holy Eucharist, the cross, submission to God's will and victory through suffering borne courageously. The latter we can see most of all in two poems *"Beneath the Palm – on Cross and Altar"* as well as Anna's *"Illness and Operation Poem"*, which Father Rieger confirmed in writing[66].

---

66 The two poems are found in the appendix of this volume, on pages 61 and 63.

In addition to her apostolate of suffering, her needle and her pen, we must not fail to see another one, that is, the apostolate of intercessory prayer. Anna Schäffer made herself the "load –bearer" of humanity for others. Like a letter carrier, she wanted to come before the Saviour each day laden with the large and small bundles of her supplicants and after Holy Communion lay them at His feet[67]. And she also wanted to continue this apostolate of intercession even after her death. Already in 1916 she wrote to her friend Anna Bortenhauser the words that would become famous:

"And if some day I shall go up there for eternity I shall be so happy to get to where Jesus is – I shall be a real intercessor for all of you!"[68]

Anna kept her promise. The countless prayers granted since her death and attributed by the faithful to her intercession before God are an undeniable sign of this. Even after her death she wanted to be near to humankind and understand them in their cares.
Once a visitor expressed her regret at Anna's bedside that after her death she could no longer come to visit her and complained with concern: ‚Nandl [an affectionate nickname for Anna], what will we do when you are no longer here?' Anna responded with these consoling words:

"Just go to my grave, I will certainly understand you!"[69]

Until this day Anna Schäffer's grave is the goal of thousands who can discover there her compassion, her understanding, and most of all her nearness in interceding for them. On the day of her burial Father Rieger shared with many people his conviction of the deceased's enduring intercession before God.

"What this victim soul suffered as an extraordinary sacrifice with the Saviour's special grace is known only to the omniscient God, and if instead of patient suffering on earth, from heaven this victim soul can provide us with blessings and thus can remain known to people, we unworthy humans cannot judge; that is up to the Lord's grace and the Church's decision. As painful as the death of this victim soul is for us, we may find comfort at her grave, knowing that her pain-racked body has found rest, and that this soul now so near to God will remain our great intercessor and will continue to pray for us in our need."[70]

---

67 Cf. „Im Leiden habe ich Dich lieben gelernt!". Die Schriften Anna Schäffers. Dokumentiert von Emmeram H. Ritter, Regensburg 1999, p. 368.
68 Anna Schäffer, Letter of 18 November 1916, in: BKR Abt. C.A.S. Proc. sup. perqu. Scriptorum S. I–IV D. 1–43 K. 9 (quoted from the original).
69 Cf. Letter of L. A. from K., 26 July 1999, in: BKR Abt. C.A.S. Transcriptions: Thoughts and Memories/ Dream book/ Poetry/ Accounts concerning AS K. 16.
70 Remarks at the graveside of the virgin Anna Schäfer (sic!), who suffered and sacrificed for 25 years in Mindelstetten. Given on 8 October 1925 by Rev. Father Karl Rieger. Habbel Brothers' Press, Regensburg, in: BKR Abt. C.A.S. Acts 1921–1925 K. 19.

Anna Schäffer's first grave in the former parish cemetery in Mindelstetten, very close to the Parish Church of St. Nicholas. *(Photographic archives)*

Special Attention of the Children, Young People and Villagers

We cannot fail to mention a few loving attentions that Anna Schäffer experienced from the villagers. They brightened her days filled with suffering and pain and show the appreciation of her fellow beings, who tried to involve her in the events of village life and let her participate in them. Anna herself recounts to her friend Anna Bortenhauser a flag dedication ceremony in the summer of 1919. At noon on the holiday the parade bearing the newly dedicated flag came to her. The musicians played a song beneath Anna's window to give her a little joy. The next day a lively group of village children came to her room to continue the celebration with childlike merriment and recite for her the poems they had learned. In gratitude for their enthusiasm Anna gave the children a tissue paper streamer for their flag and aroused great joy among the little ones. Anna was always ready to give her support and involved herself in preparations to the point of exhaustion, making paper roses and bows which, because of the work in the fields, the people of the village had no time to do[71].

Anna Schäffer on her sickbed, surrounded by children. (Oil painting by Prechtl 1999 / Photo by Zacharias)

71 Cf. Anna Schäffer's account in her letter of 10 September 1919 in: „Im Leiden habe ich Dich lieben gelernt!". Die Schriften Anna Schäffers. Dokumentiert von Emmeram H. Ritter, Regensburg 1999, p. 195.

Another event that Anna Schäffer mentioned with great joy and gratitude in her letters was a surprise given her on 26 December 1922, St. Stephen's Day, and which she likewise reported to her friend. Following a local practice after Christmas a Christmas tree raffle took place. The proceeds were usually given to restore the club treasury. The lads from the Mindelstetten veterans' association came up with the idea of presenting this type of Christmas tree to Anna and it was auctioned off several times, thereby increasing its value greatly. The suggestion met the approval of all. They also wanted to give Anna a sum of money they had collected. The village head teacher spoke about it in the inn. With selfless joy the young children, whose number filled Ann's room completely, delivered a richly decorated Christmas tree, with a good sum of money, and coffee and washing powder. Each of them took her hand and, upon parting, said, "Nandl, we won't forget you" and added that they would gladly try to grant any wish she might have. The last of the youngsters gave her a further sum of money to pay for the periodicals she so greatly enjoyed. They also brought Anna eggs, meal and even a large load of wood to supply her needs. Anna considered this a great honour and even enjoyed the article published in the local newspaper[72].

The love and affection of the village children was a special delight for Anna Schäffer. They often came to visit her, asking many questions and surrounding her bed. They also wanted to carry the cross at her funeral, accompany her coffin with candles and in a childlike way promised to decorate her grave with flowers when she died. Especially in the summer the children heaped flowers on Anna's bed, as she herself reports[73].

However, certainly the most beautiful experience for Anna during her long illness and her pain-filled days was her visit to the so-called "Altötting Chapel" at the edge of Mindelstetten on 4 October 1916 and, a few days later, a holy Mass in the parish church. With deep gratitude Anna recalls both events. She was carried to the chapel in an easy chair and there, despite her weakness, she was able to participate in praying the whole Rosary. So too on 13 October 1916 she experienced an unspeakable joy. For many years she had nourished the secret desire to be able to participate in a Mass. This wish was now quickly and unexpectedly fulfilled. In the morning they carried her to Mass and so she was able to receive Holy Communion in the parish church. They left her sitting in an easy chair quite near the tabernacle. And although she was very weak, she was still able to last for the entire Mass, even though ten years earlier she had been carried to church and was able to endure for a few minutes, because she felt so sick[74].

---

[72] Cf. Anna Schäffer's detailed report in her letter of December 1922, in: „Im Leiden habe ich Dich lieben gelernt!". Die Schriften Anna Schäffers. Dokumentiert von Emmeram H. Ritter, Regensburg 1999, S. 336 f.
[73] Cf. Anna Schäffer, Letter of 11 November 1917, in: BKR Abt. C.A.S. Proc. sup. perqu. Scriptorum S. I–IV D. 1–43 K. 9.
[74] Cf. Anna Schäffer, Letter of 18 October 1916, in: BKR Abt. C.A.S. Proc. sup. perqu. Scriptorum S. I–IV D. 1–43 K. 9 ; also portions of letters from Anna Schäffer to Sister Tatona, in: BKR Abt. C.A.S. Proc. sup. perqu. Scriptorum D. 131 183 K. 12.

The so-called "Altöttinger Chapel" near Mindelstetten. *(Photo: Tautz)*

Her Last Years, Blessed Death and Fulfilment in God

On the feast of St. Mark (25 April) 1923, according to her own report, during a Good Friday vision Anna Schäffer experienced the sufferings of Christ on the Mount of Olives. She fell into a rigour that lasted eight hours, and they feared she was dying. According to Father Rieger, the entire time her eyes were fixed on an image of the Ecce Homo[75]. The record of the Good Friday vision still exists in a shorthand original that Anna Schäffer dictated to Rosa Imlauer.

"On 25 April 1923 I saw the dear Saviour and he showed me a crown of thorns and all over the points a drop of blood hung. – Then suddenly I was in the Garden of Olives. There I saw the dear Saviour pray and sweat blood. The apostles were behind Him and bent over asleep. I also saw how the dear Saviour was taken prisoner and how the first time the guards fell to the ground and after a little while bound his hands and hauled Him away. I also saw how they dragged Him before Pilate and before the High Court. I saw Him suffering so in prison. It was so dark and cold and He was so alone. I saw Him led back to Pilate and as He came out of there, I saw Him laden with the heavy cross. First he went along a wide road, then they turned into a narrow alley and then through a gate. In front of the gate He fell so painfully to earth. Then the procession went up Mount Calvary. I saw how the dear Saviour was nailed to the cross and how on the cross He died. I saw how from behind the cross Saint (Mary) Magdalene clung to His feet. The dear Mother of God and Saint John were also there. On Mount Calvary and on the Mount of Olives I was able to feel pain all over me. It came to me that our death must be only a tiny part of what the dear Saviour suffered for us. As I looked on, this lasted from four o'clock in the afternoon until midnight on 25 April 1923."[76]

From that day onwards Anna's condition grew worse. Her legs were completely crippled, accompanied by spinal pain, painful cramps and in the end by rectal cancer. Remarkable, however, according to Father Rieger's report, despite these extremely weakening cramps Anna was still able to receive Holy Communion and after receiving she made her Act of Thanksgiving. Due to a fall from her bed in mid-August 1925 the she suffered a brain injury that affected her speech[77]. During the last weeks of her life Anna often asked the visiting parish priest for his priestly blessing[78].

---

76 Cf. Rev. Carl Rieger, Letter of 5 February 1926, in: BKR Abt. C.A.S. Acts 1926–1930 K. 20.
77 Good Friday vision, 1923. Written by Rosa Imlauer according to the dictation of Anna Schäffer; quoted literally here from the transcription of the shorthand original, in: BKR Abt. C.A.S. Proc. sup. perqu. Scriptorum D. 131–183 K. 12.
78 Cf. Rev. Carl Rieger, Report on Anna Schäffer of 4 February 1929, in: BKR Abt. C.A.S. Acts 1926–1930 K. 20.
79 Cf. Rev. Carl Rieger, Letter of 5 February 1926, in: BKR Abt. C.A.S. Acts 1926–1930 K. 20.

On the morning of 5 October 1925, the day of her death, she received Holy Communion for the last time. Father Rieger describes her death in great detail:
"In the morning of the Feast of the Rosary the landlord's daughter died; she found resignation to God's will in the example and prayer of Anna Schäffer. Upon hearing of her death, Anna Schäffer said: 'Look where we have ended up!' Some claim to have heard Anna state that they would die together. In the morning the one who was deathly weak received Holy Communion with her usual devotion. At one o'clock in the afternoon I visited her and found her very weak. At three o'clock I was called for the prayers for the dying. It was truly an ecstasy. [...]. At 5:30 I spoke to her again and when I explained that I was going to the church to pray the rosary for the landlord's daughter, she nodded. At 6:30 I returned to her deathbed, where she had her gaze fixed on the picture of the Ecce Homo, perhaps praying silently. I considered her weakness no different than what she had often experienced and left. The others said that when I left she turned towards me as if to say something. I was hardly even 100 meters away from the house when she stopped breathing and they told me that she had been freed from her suffering. I immediately returned and found that blessed one dead, but could not believe it [...]. Many people, especially the young folk, came to her funeral. The people would have gladly carried off and cut up every possible memento had they not been prevented from doing so. They expected some kind of beatification ceremony from the funeral homily; however, I had to limit myself to the many graces she received during her life of suffering and that the deceased had enjoyed an abundance of God's grace."[79]

Anna was a member of the Third Order and was therefore buried in the habit of a Franciscan Tertiary, as a still extant photo shows. We know from a letter that she wrote to a friend that she had her "wedding gown" blessed on the Feast of the Porziuncola in 1919 in order *"to be able to lie down in the quiet peace of the grave as a poor Franciscan [...]. Now I need nothing more, my travelling bag is totally ready!"*[80]. On a Feast of the Porziuncola she joined the Third Order and she had had her habit for many years before she had it blessed. Through her decision to join the Third Order of Saint Francis, Anna Schäffer demonstrated her appreciation for the poverty[81] which this saint modelled in imitation of Jesus and which was quite close to the circumstances of her own life. Therefore, in her own words, since 1919 Anna had been ready for her journey to eternity; six years later Christ called her to Himself, her heavenly Bridegroom.

---

79 Rev. Carl Rieger, Report on Anna Schäffer of 4 February 1929 (Transcription), in: BKR Abt. C.A.S. Acts 1926–1930 K. 20.
80 Anna Schäffer, Letter of 12 August 1919, in: BKR Abt. C.A.S. Proc. sup. perqu. Scriptorum D. 44–76 K. 10 (quoted from the original).
81 Cf. Rev. Carl Rieger, Report on Anna Schäffer of 4 February 1929, in: BKR Abt. C.A.S. Acts 1926–1930 K. 20.

Anna Schäffer, laid out for burial in the habit of a Franciscan tertiary. *(Photographic archives)*

On 8 October 1925 with a great participation of the population, she was buried in the cemetery in Mindelstetten. Father Rieger, who for so many years had been her spiritual director, was personally convinced of the holy life of his parishioner, as can still be seen today in a brief note in the registry of Anna Schäffer's death. Where it asks for the occupation of the deceased, he added in pencil: "Sancta" – a "saint"[82]. As her spiritual director for many years, he noted that in Anna Schäffer he had met a saint and he was allowed to be her spiritual companion. However, humility and obedience not to anticipate the Church's judgment in the matter, as well as his pastoral shrewdness, kept him from openly expressing to the gathered mourners his opinion and his firm inner conviction. The Church has now raised Anna Schäffer to the honour of the altars and the future proved Father Carl Rieger right. Anna led a holy life. She allowed herself to be led by God's will, even in her frustrated plans for her life, to a painful sickbed and the want of poverty.

Her siblings had a simple tombstone placed over her grave. Father Rieger chose for Anna, as he himself reported, a grave beneath the pulpit of the former parish

---

82 Cf. Georg Schwaiger, Anna Schäffer von Mindelstetten. Ein Leben in der Gnade Gottes, Regensburg, 4th edition 2000, p. 13.

church, which had been demolished in April 1905 during his term in office[83]. Since Anna Schäffer's death the procession of pilgrims to her grave, which Bishop Antonius von Henle (1906–1927) later had finished with brickwork[84], has never ended. After the expression of the wishes of many of the faithful, Bishop Dr. Rudolf Graber of Regensburg († 1992) finally approved the transfer of the remains of the Servant of God from the cemetery into the parish church of Mindelstetten and the opening of the diocesan process for her beatification. Pope John Paul II decided for the heroic level of her virtues on 11 July 1995 when he consented to the publication of the decree of Anna Schäffer's heroic virtues. The miracle necessary for her beatification was recognized with a decree of 3 July 1998. In preparation for the beatification, on 30 January 1999 the canonical recognition of her remains and their subsequent translation was conducted by Bishop Manfred Müller of Regensburg. At that time her relics were transferred from the previous grave site in the southern nave of the former parish church in Mindelstetten and ceremonially laid in a new grave in the central nave. On 7 March 1999 in St. Peter's Basilica in Rome, Pope John Paul II beatified the poor, suffering servant girl, Anna Schäffer. A second miracle attributed to her intercession was recognised by Pope Benedict XVI on 19 December 2011. He will canonise Anna Schäffer on 21 October 2012 in Rome and place her before the eyes of the universal Church as a shining example.

Bishop Rudolf Graber (1962–1982) of Regensburg at the close of the diocesan process, with the prepared and sealed acts ready for transport to Rome. (Photo: Starzinger)

---

84 Cf. Rev. Carl Rieger, Report on Anna Schäffer of 4 February 1929, in: BKR Abt. C.A.S. Acts 1926–1930 K. 20; also Ritter Emmeram H., Anna Schäffer. Eine Selige aus Bayern, Regensburg 2012, p. 89.
85 Cf. Rev. Carl Rieger, Letter to Bishop Michael Buchberger of 5 October 1928, in: BKR Abt. C.A.S. Acts 1926–1930 K. 20.

Anna Schäffer's grave in the central nave of the former Parish Church in Mindelstetten. (Photo: v. Götz)

Appreciation for and the Meaning of Anna Schäffer's Life's Work

In his report on Anna Schäffer's suffering, **Father Carl Rieger** emphasises that he had been an eyewitness "to a life of heroic suffering" and "can give every assurance that it is only the whole truth of her hidden suffering and life of grace, and that all he ever wanted was to be the fortunate director of a spiritual life that was so greatly graced by God"[85]. It was his conviction that her humble bearing of her suffering had made of Anna a "victim soul for God"[86], for her own salvation and a blessing for mankind. From Father Rieger's remarks at Anna Schäffer's grave we readily see the renown for holiness that the deceased enjoyed among the local populace.

Photo from 1927. (Photographic archives)

"Not with science could the departed raise her voice amid the tumult of the world and many were happy to hear amid the suffering of this valley of tears, words of comfort from the mouth of a poor maiden who could speak in the love of the Saviour; indeed, many were edified to see the peaceful joy of the Lord's way to heaven that brightened the eyes of this woman who was able to plumb the depths of the wisdom of the cross. We are standing at the grave of the virtuous virgin Anna Schäffer, the daughter of a carpenter from Mindelstetten. At the age of 43 her earthly shell will be lowered into the grave to await the resurrection when her body, worn down by years of suffering, will one day be united with her soul, shining brightly like that of the Saviour's body. What shall I say at this grave? I must ask, what should I not say at this place of eternal rest, what many would like to hear, but which only the future can establish with the Church's decision"[87].

Her long life of suffering was "a life in and according to faith"[88], said Father Rieger. "In 25 years I never heard a complaint"[89]. When Anna recognised that God had not called her to religious life, "the promises of faith were the only goal she strove for"[90].

---

[85] Rev. Carl Rieger, Report on Anna Schäffer of 4 February 1929 (Transcription), in: BKR Abt. C.A.S. Acts 1926–1930 K. 20.
[86] Rev. Carl Rieger, Report on Anna Schäffer of 4 February 1929 (Transcription), in: BKR Abt. C.A.S. Acts 1926–1930 K. 20.
[87] Words at the graveside of the virgin Anna Schäfer (sic!), who in Mindelstetten suffered and sacrificed for 25 years. Delivered on 8 October 1925 by Rev. Fath Karl Rieger. Printed by the Habbel Brothers, Regensburg, in: BKR Abt. C.A.S. Acts 1921–1925 K. 19.
[88] Rev. Carl Rieger, Report on Anna Schäffer of 4 February 1929 (Transcription), in: BKR Abt. C.A.S. Acts 1926–1930 K. 20.
[89] Rev. Carl Rieger, Report on Anna Schäffer of 4 February 1929 (Transcription), in: BKR Abt. C.A.S. Acts 1926–1930 K. 20.
[90] Rev. Carl Rieger, Report on Anna Schäffer of 4 February 1929 (Transcription), in: BKR Abt. C.A.S. Acts 1926–1930 K. 20.

In 1980 the noted dogmatic theologian from Regensburg, **Professor Dr. Johann Baptist Auer** (1910–1989) in his capacity as an expert witness, offered his judgment of Anna Schäffer's written work, and described her personality in the following way:

"Because of the greatness of this human life in the light of the Christian view of the world, because of the depth of her expiratory suffering and the height of her total human self-offering, because of the earnestness of her heroic devotion and the sheen of grace shining forth in this life, because of the inexhaustibility of this Christian life and the spiritual health that is revealed precisely through and in this life totally defined by the love of Jesus, may the holy Church raise her worthy daughter to the honours of the altar"[91].

(Photographic archives)

On the eve of Anna Schäffer's beatification, to prepare the pilgrims for the event, in the Roman Basilica of St. Paul Outside the Walls the Prefect of the Congregation for the Doctrine of the Faith **Cardinal Joseph Ratzinger (Pope Benedict XVI)** preached a homily in which he explained the significance of Anna Schäffer's life's work for our time in a memorable manner[92]. He said that during the 25 years of her suffering she made a "great journey inwards and upwards" and therefore in the night of suffering she found "the day of Jesus Christ". Anna Schäffer "immersed herself in the mystery of the suffering Christ, and became a fellow sufferer with Him who suffered for our sake." So, in the end, he said, people no longer came to her to console her, but to be consoled by her. And finally the Cardinal led his listeners into the mystery of suffering, as she herself experienced it, saying:

"[...] naturally we must do everything to soothe and alleviate suffering. However, anyone who claims that we do not need to do any more is foolish. Because it is so important, and remains so, to learn suffering and find one's self in it. Suffering and humanity are indivisible. There is no love without a readiness to deny one's self, without the necessity of constantly tolerating the other's otherness anew. There is no love without the pain of change. This is the only way one can mature. There is no faithfulness without pain and the patience of the change that we need. And if only the person who has changed much can grow rich, then truly only those who

---

91 Judgment of merit in the process for the beatification of the Servant of god, Anna Schäffer, born on 18 February 1882 in Mindelstetten (Bavaria, Diocese of Regensburg) based on her own writings, signed by Johann Auer, in: BKR Abt. C.A.S. Proc. sup. perqu. Scriptorum D. 1–43 K. 9.
92 Dem Menschen helfen, das Leiden zu erlernen und anzunehmen. Homily of Cardinal Joseph Ratzinger at Saint Paul's Outside the Walls of Rome (6 March 1999), in: Selige Anna Schäffer von Mindelstetten/Bayern December 2000, Letter 38, edited by the Department for Causes of Beatification and Canonisation of the Episcopal Consistory of the Diocese of Regensburg 2000, pp. 10–17.

have accepted suffering and learned to accept it truly can become rich. The one who can no longer suffer can no longer be compassionate. And the one who can no longer be compassionate can no longer love. A world in which no one can sink in suffering becomes a cold and cruel world."[93]

And in reference to Pope St. Pius X Cardinal Ratzinger added:

"When Pius X was still a country parish priest in the Veneto (Region of Italy) he composed a handwritten catechism for schools. We still have it today and in it we find the question: Why did the Son of God become man? The surprisingly strange answer: In order to teach us suffering. The Veneto was terribly poor at that time. Poverty and inadequate diet caused many illnesses and premature death. Suffering was all about. Only the person who knew how to suffer could live. And learning to suffer was the first step toward liberation, self-realisation, inner freedom. Thanks be to God things are not like that for us. In a large part of the world it is still so. However, for us it is still true that if we do not learn to suffer, we do not learn to live and we do not learn to love. And thus Anna Schäffer stands before us, the one who learned suffering and so teaches us to live."[94]

Cardinal Joseph Ratzinger (Pope Benedict XVI) during a homily in the Roman Basilica of St. Paul-Outside-the-Walls on 6 March 1999, the eve of Anna Schäffer's Beatification. (Photographic archives)

---

[93] Dem Menschen helfen, das Leiden zu erlernen und anzunehmen. Homily of Cardinal Joseph Ratzinger at Saint Paul's Outside the Walls of Rome (6 March 1999), in: Selige Anna Schäffer von Mindelstetten/Bayern December 2000, Letter 38, edited by the Department for Causes of Beatification and Canonisation of the Episcopal Consistory of the Diocese of Regensburg 2000, pp. 14–15.

[94] Dem Menschen helfen, das Leiden zu erlernen und anzunehmen. Homily of Cardinal Joseph Ratzinger at Saint Paul's Outside the Walls of Rome (6 March 1999), in: Selige Anna Schäffer von Mindelstetten/Bayern December 2000, Letter 38, published by the Department for Causes of Beatification and Canonisation of the Episcopal Consistory of the Diocese of Regensburg 2000, pp. 15–16.

Pope John Paul II paid tribute to Anna Schäffer on 7 March 1999, the day of her beatification in St. Peter's Basilica in Rome, when in his homily he repeated her words about her "workshop of suffering", the three "keys to heaven", but also her apostolate for the salvation of her neighbour. The Pope said that the Heart of Jesus, surmounted by flames depicted as ears of wheat, will be Anna Schäffer's symbol.

"The more her life's journey became a journey of suffering, the more clearly she recognised that illness and frailty can be the lines on which God writes his Gospel. She called her sickroom a "workshop of suffering", to resemble the cross of Christ ever more closely. She spoke of three keys to heaven that God had given her [...]. Precisely in the most intense pain Anna Schäffer realized that every Christian is responsible for his neighbour's salvation.. For this purpose she used the pen. Her sickbed was the cradle of an extensive letter-writing apostolate. She used what was left of her strength to do embroidery work and in this way gave joy to others. In her letters and in her handiwork her favourite motif was the heart of Jesus as the symbol of God's love. She did not depict the flames of Jesus' heart as tongues of fire, but as ears of wheat. The reference to the Eucharist, which Anna Schäffer received from her parish priest every day, is unmistakable. The heart of Jesus, as she portrayed it, will thus be the symbol of this new blessed"[95].

Pope John Paul II during the Beatification Mass on 7 March 1999.   (Photo: L'Osservatore Romano)

---

[95] John Paul II. Homily for the Beatification Mass in St. Peter's Basilica, 7 March 1999, part five. English translation provided by Vatican Information Services, © Copyright 1999 - Libreria Editrice Vaticana.

In his address in Mindelstetten during the solemn Mass of Thanksgiving for the beatification of Anna Schäffer several weeks after the celebrations in Rome, **Diocesan Ordinary Bishop Manfred Müller** emphasized the transforming power of suffering. The new Blessed understood how to change suffering and pain into something good. With trust in Jesus, who by his death and dying redeemed us from the meaninglessness of suffering, we Christians are borne by faith that from suffering roses can bloom.

"We dare to point out that someone like Anna Schäffer was made to change the "why?" of suffering into a "what for?" and a "for what purpose?". Suffering at its deepest level can have meaning only if it is borne for another. The suffering of every good mother and grandmother can be a blessing for the children, for the grandchildren. Suffering has a deep power to change, especially when it is viewed, as Romano Guardini put it: 'To change the burden into goodness.' [...] The burden of her life, a quarter of a century confined to bed, racked with pain, she [Anna Schäffer] changed into goodness. Goodness shone from her. Everyone who came to her, children and adults alike, was moved by this goodness, by her inherent goodness. [...] She changed her burden into goodness--that was her life's work, in the power of the Holy Spirit. [...]. Through His suffering and death Jesus conquered death. He redeemed us from the meaninglessness of suffering and also opened for us the path through suffering into glory. There is no perfect answer to the question of why, but we live through the power of faith, so that roses can bloom from suffering."[96]

During the Beatification Mass: Bishop Manfred Müller of Regensburg asks Pope John Paul II for the Beatification of Anna Schäffer. (Photo: L'Osservatore Romano)

---

96 Die Last in Güte verwandeln – Der Herr bleibt bei uns in seinem Wort, in seinem Sakrament und in seinen Heiligen. Address of Bishop Manfred Müller of the Diocese of Regensburg during the Pontifical Mass of Thanksgiving for the beatification of Anna Schäffer in Mindelstetten (Easter Monday, 5 April 1999), in: Selige Anna Schäffer von Mindelstetten/Bayern December 1999, Letter 36, published by the Department for Causes of Beatification and Canonisation of the Episcopal Consistory of the Diocese of Regensburg 1999, pp. 12–14.

During his usual visits to Mindelstetten for the Days of Prayer for the beatification of Anna Schäffer, **Diocesan Ordinary Bishop Gerhard Ludwig Müller** repeatedly explained her meaning for the people of our day. In her God Himself reveals the power of His grace, which does not fail people even in suffering and need. Anna Schäffer is a question for each of us if we, like her, unite the suffering of our life with Christ and so remain His follower, in order to be one with Him each day.

"Considered from a purely human point of view, here we have a gathering of people who have good memories of Anna Schäffer and are amazed at the patience and human strength with which she bore the great misfortunes of her life and was not broken down by adversity. However, this purely human view is not enough. [...]. God Himself reveals His glory in Anna Schäffer, the transforming power of His grace, the consoling power of the Holy Spirit who does not let people sink in suffering and need, but binds them intimately with Christ crucified. Through His suffering on the cross and His Resurrection He opened for us the gates of eternal life. This is what we see in Anna Schäffer's life, in her spiritual conduct, in her inner maturation, what really matters in a short human life, marked by suffering and death. Unlike all other living things, the human being has not only a mere earthly goal. [...]. The life of Blessed Anna Schäffer shows us that through our life and action, through our good works, we can make God's power and the Kingdom of God's grace visible in this world. If in our sickness and old age we can no longer do outward things, so we may interiorly offer our suffering in imitation of the crucified Lord."[97]

Bishop Gerhard Ludwig Müller of Regensburg at an "Anna Schäffer Day of Prayer" in Mindelstetten. (Photo: Feldmann)

"This [Anna Schäffer's] example is also a question for us: How would I act in such a situation, with a difficult fate of my own? With anger against God? With inner doubt? Despair? Arguing against fate? Or as a believer would I look upon Christ on the cross, who has suffered for me and borne my pain? [...]. In this sense Anna Schäffer accepted her suffering and united

---

[97] Bishop Gerhard Ludwig Müller of Regensburg, Selige Anna Schäffer, bitte für unsere Priester! – Anna-Schäffer-Prayer Day on 26 July 2009, in: Selige Anna Schäffer von Mindelstetten/Bayern December 2009, Letter 56, published by the Department for Causes of Beatification and Canonisation of the Episcopal Consistory of the Diocese of Regensburg 2009, p. 22 ff.

it with that of Jesus Christ. She offered it to open up her heart and the hearts of all in view of Christ on the cross, in view of his salvation-bringing wounds. Through her prayer apostolate and her wise counsel she helped many people to find Christ. [...]. It may also be due to the prayer of Blessed Anna Schäffer and many saints that in difficult situations people find courage and that in contemplating the crucified Lord they find the strength to help their fellow man. In this we have the deepest sense of the word "Church" [...]. The example of Blessed Anna Schäffer and all the saints should lead us not only to believe in the existence of God, but to place our whole life in Christ's discipleship." [98]

'Come to me, all you who labour and are burdened, and I will give you rest. Take my yoke upon you and learn from me, for I am meek and humble of heart; and you will find rest for your selves. For my yoke is easy, and my burden light.' (Mt 11:28-30). These words of Jesus are not just for the apostles 2,000 years ago, but today are also for us who must struggle with life's burdens or those who – like Blessed Anna Schäffer – must bear difficult physical suffering without any prospect of recovery in this earthly journey. That confronts us with the question: Why after all is there suffering in this world? How should we react to it? Suffering can lead a person to protest against God, or even lead him astray, to turn entirely from God. How can a good God allow suffering anyhow? The fact is often overlooked that God Himself took on our suffering in His son, Jesus Christ. Jesus bore our pain, our need, our mortal agony to the altar of the cross, on which he offered Himself for the salvation of the world, so that from his wounds we might receive redemption and salvation and this world's suffering would be interiorly changed and can no longer serve as a protest against God; rather, Jesus' suffering becomes a sign for us that we can rely with total confidence on God. We can become one each day with the crucified and risen Christ and unite our suffering with His suffering. Then his resurrection becomes present and effective in us and through the hope that He has given us. Thus we are led into the centre and foundation of our Christian faith: Christ among us: HE is our hope for glory!" [99]

---

[98] Bishop Gerhard Ludwig Müller of Regensburg, Als gläubige Christen aufschauen zum gekreuzigten Herrn – Anna-Schäffer-Prayer Day on 26 July 2010: in Selige Anna Schäffer von Mindelstetten/Bayern December 2010, Letter 58, published by the Department for Causes of Beatification and Canonisation of the Episcopal Consistory of the Diocese of Regensburg 2010, p 21 ff.

[99] Bishop Gerhard Ludwig Müller of Regensburg, Wahre Reform der Church bedeutet immer Erneuerung in Jesus Christus! – Anna-Schäffer-Prayer Day on 26 July 2011, in: Selige Anna Schäffer von Mindelstetten/Bayern December 2011, Letter 60, published by the Department for Causes of Beatification and Canonisation of the Episcopal Consistory of the Diocese of Regensburg 2011, p. 20 ff.

O mein Jesus, hier knie ich vor dir –
Herr Herz, bist Du zufrieden mit mir? –
Und was in heutiger Zeit ich hab –
Ob Gnade vor dir es gefunden hat? –
O Herr, Du siehst in mein Herz hinein –
Du siehst wie ich möchte mein Leben dir weihn –
Du siehst, dass mein einziges Sehnen ist –
Dir, Herr, zu beweisen, wie lieb Du mir bist –
O mein Jesus, hier knie ich vor dir –
Und hab eine Bitte, erfülle sie mir –
Mir alles zu nehmen was mir noch gefällt –
Mir alles zu geben was Bitteres mir fällt –
O Herr Du siehst in das Herz mir hinein –
Du siehst wie ich selbstsüchtig und Sünde doch –
Du siehst aber auch das mein Sehnen es ist –
Jesu allein zu sterben was Du Herr nicht bist –
O mein Jesus, hier knie ich vor dir –
Was soll ich dir geben? Was willst Du von mir?
Mein Blut und mein Leben? Wie gäb ich so froh? –
Gesundheit und Ehr? – Sag, willst Du es so? –
Und doch wäre das alles zu wenig zu schlecht –
Nein Herr nur dein Wille und Kreuz ist es recht –
Den blinden Gehorsam, den willst du es ist –
Du lass mich dir zeigen wie lieb du mir bist –
O mein Jesus, hier knie ich vor dir –
Zwei einzige Bitten erfülle sie mir: –
Mach mich mir als alles – gering und klein –
Lass jedermann tugend vollkommner sein –
Lass keine sich mehr in Gehorsam als ich –
Anfass im Altern, nach glühender dich –
Gehorsam und Liebe zur heiligsten –
das danken zu den Füßen sich hinab wälzt sich"

First page of Anna's letter to Anna Bortenhauser, 6 September 1918. (Photo: Horoba)

Concluding Observations

An encounter with Anna Schäffer's life faces us with the question of the meaning, or even more, of the value of suffering. Anna grasped and lived in a personal way what we read in the New Testament Letter to the Colossians: "Now I rejoice in my sufferings for your sake, and in my flesh I am filling up what is lacking in the afflictions of Christ on behalf of his body, which is the Church" (Col 1: 24). She recognised that it was her God-given vocation to pray and suffer in union with Christ for the Church and most of all for the conversion of sinners[100]. She remained true to this calling unto death.

In light of the indescribable suffering and pain that Anna Schäffer had to endure and which she bore in union with Christ, we can only look at her in wonder and silently bow. We may, however, draw something out of the richness of this life marked by suffering and yet so richly blessed. In Anna Schäffer we find fulfilled what the Psalmist expressed in the comforting words: "My God, in you I trust;...No one is disgraced who waits for you" (Ps 25:2,3). In the purification of her life Anna was not disgraced, because she trusted in Christ, the Saviour, who in his Eucharistic sacrament stirred her with his loving kindness. Strengthened by Him, she was ready to let go of her plans for love of God and to accept the mystery of the cross of Christ in her life willingly, even gratefully.

The Spanish Trappist Rafael Arnáiz Barón (1911–1938), Anna Schäffer's contemporary, who was canonised by Pope Benedict XVI in October 2009, once wrote: "God leads me by the hand through a land in which there are tears, wars and misery. He places me near the cross and while with His glance he indicates all of this, He says to me: 'All is mine; do not hold it in contempt!'"[101]. Anna Schäffer, too, was placed by God near the cross. She did not hold it in contempt, but by gazing on Jesus Christ, the crucified Redeemer, she learned to love the cross as His sign and possession.

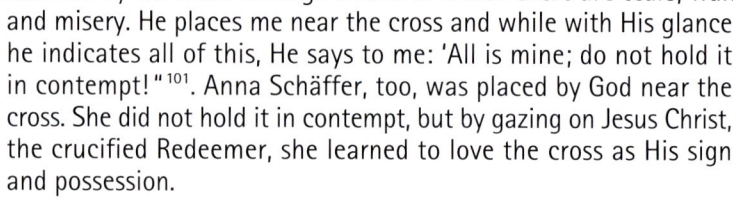

Every saint is like an open portal that sends God's light streaming into the darkness of this world.

---

100 Cf. Anna Schäffer, Letter of 29 January 1919, in: BKR Abt. C.A.S. Proc. sup. perqu. Scriptorum D. 44–76 K. 10.
101 The German text of the quotation was taken from: Urs Buhlmann, Geschärfter Sinn fürs Endliche. Der junge spanische Trappist Rafael lehrt uns: Die Gottergebenheit beim Gemüse-Schälen, in: Die Tagespost, Edition of 19 January 2012/Nr. 8, S. 6

Anna Schäffer is such a portal for all those tried by sickness, poverty and suffering. She shows that even the lot and fate of an incurable illness can be borne with trust in Christ, who Himself became a Suffering One, a Fellow Sufferer and Supporter in order to give us the consolation of His divine presence in pain and death. He invites every person to participate in his redemptive action through his or her own personal cross[102].

Anna Schäffer accepted this invitation from Christ. She fulfilled her "mission of suffering". Thus she became and remains a witness to love. Over her life marked by illness, suffering and poverty towers the great Christian truth that even in suffering the person is loved by God.

Michelangelo's Pieta, Rome, St. Peter's Basilica.
(Photographic Archives)

Anna Schäffer

**MOST HOLY VIRGIN AND MOTHER OF GOD, MARY,
QUEEN OF ALL SAINTS,
HEALTH OF THE SICK AND COMFORTER OF THE AFFLICTED,
PRAY FOR US!**

---

102 Cf. Benedict XVI: Blessing of the sick at the end of Mass in Fatima, Portugal on 13 May 2010, English translation taken from the Holy See's web-site: www.vatican.va

Anna Schäffer's Poems

Corpus Christi Wishes

So far from my Lord to be -
And not to be able to look Him in the eye –
Separated from Him through so many rows -
those going for the Corpus Christi celebration. -
Tears come to my eyes -
great nostalgia fills my heart -
O Lord, when I am not near You -
Everything is pain and suffering for me. -

Little bird, with your rapid wings -
I so envy your happiness -
Would I were only in your place. -
Nothing could hold me back from the Lord -
I would fly right up to the monstrance -
And drink my fill of its light -
In the sweet shimmer of its beauty -

You can see Him – I cannot!

O little flower lying along the way -
How unspeakably rich you are -
That you can adorn his footfall -
Where is there such a joy as yours? -
O God, how gladly I would die -
I would only lie at Your feet -
Blessed still by my Lord -,

You can see Him – I cannot!

Oh banner fluttering so happily -
waving in the bright sunshine
proceeding before and following after Him -
You pennants, large and small -
Oh would that I too had the happiness -
Of gazing at the Lord's countenance -
How gladly I would go along with you -

You can see Him – I cannot!

*And you first of all, O Angel of the Lord –
Whose hand the Saviour raises and holds –
Tell me! Is it not true that the whole world –
Is far removed from you in this journey? –
As if your heart were already at home –
Up there in heaven's light? –
Your happiness – no word can express it –*

You carry the Lord – I cannot!

*And yet I can – and I want to, too –
As long as my heart beats in me –
And I want to until my last breath –
As long as I still have a pulse –
I want to carry Him, the dear Lord –
I want only to see Him – in pure love –
Even if in my body I am far from Him –
My heart shall be near Him always –*

*O Jesus, draw us all to You –
Yes, draw us to Your Heart –
Save me a place at Your side –
O Lord, in joy and pain –
You know it – I cannot live
if anything separates me from You –
Keep my heart O Lord, so close –
quite close – in Your Holy Sacrament!*[103]

---

103 Anna Schäffer, Letter of 14 June 1919, in: BKR Abt. C.A.S. Proc. sup. perqu. Scriptorum D. 44–76 K. 10 (quoted from the original).

The Sun Has Not Yet Awaken

The sun has not yet awaken -
The world rests as if in dream -
Draw me in spirit with all your might -
To my supreme Good -
Draw me to the tabernacle -
Replete with warming love -
How could I begin the day
Without being with You -
O Lord, at Your feet -
Your sickly child does kneel -
Turn your eyes towards me -
In mercy, love and gentleness -
Stretch out Your hand and bless me -
From Your holy shrine -
Step out of it and come and stay -
Deep within my heart -
I would so gladly receive You -
In Holy Communion -
Because, in the pleasure of my Lord
I am already enjoying heaven -
I eat Your Flesh – I drink Your Blood -
And so I remain in You -
And You, my God, my supreme good
Remain miraculously with me -
Then I live – no longer I -
You alone are my life -
You think and speak and act through me -
You direct all that I do -
Oh wondrous union -
Oh life that is already heavenly -
Where is there a joy so great and pure
As that of Holy Communion?
And whenever I bear You in my heart
Every joy is mine -
Life's pain and joys and difficulties
Cannot be too heavy for me -
I hardly feel the bitter pain -

I notice not the want –
You raise my head and heal my heart –
O God, hidden in Bread –
Until I come before Your face –
And can joyfully bow before You –
I want to stay in spirit in that eternal Light –
a little, burning flame –
My waking hours which I there –
dedicate entirely to Him –
They are my greatest blessing indeed –
For time and all eternity! [104]

Beneath the Palm Tree – on the Cross and Altar

Beneath the palm tree – on the cross and altar–
I want always to kneel in spirit –
There alone will I in truth have the strength
to bloom tall, just like the palm trees –
There will I become like a living tree –
Planted along the streams –
That in the hallowed space of the little church –
You nourish me with the fullness of good –
Beneath the palm tree – by the priest – dedicated –
I want to suffer and work always –
I want to increase the talent the Lord loaned me –
abundantly – for His honour –
Each and every offering – large or small –
Difficult or easy – I want to make –
full of love – for heaven's sake alone –
And thus reach those palm trees –
Beneath the palm tree – there I spend –
difficult and painful hours –
I look at you – oh – from there I draw
balsam for my pain and wounds –
the cross decorating my little room –
points me to Him who bore –
a thousand times more in pain and shame

---

[104] Anna Schäffer, Letter of 10 February 1920, in: BKR Abt. C.A.S. Proc. sup. perqu. Scriptorum D. 77–130 K. 11 (quoted from the original).

then can I really complain about my cross? –
Beneath the palm tree – there I want to renew –
my bond with Jesus every day –
only to offer to him, my Chosen One, –
from my innermost depths suffering and love –
Whatever I experience – think – say – and do –
I lay lovingly at his feet
Mornings at Eucharist and at night when I rest –
My Hosanna shall greet him –
Beneath the palm tree – there I learn quite well –
to gather roses for my neighbour –
gently to forgive – even if his sharp thorns –
prick me and draw blood. –
Acts of love and words of graciousness –
I want to weave into a crown –
triumphant faith and holy – patience
are to be found only sub palma.
Beneath the palm tree - I now spend-
years and days and hours –
There I will at last run the course of them –
one day in the wounds of the Paschal Lamb
Once again I shall turn my fading gaze –
Happily to that blessed branch –
I will give back to God my soul –
so that he can show his kindness. –
Beneath the palm – my coffin can stay –
May my burial mound rise above it -
Home – to the eternal palm trees to go –
An angel will lend me its wings -
and will lead me up – to the heavenly throne –
so that with psalms of exaltation –
I can praise the Father, Spirit and Son –
Forever – then beneath the palms![105]

---

[105] Anna Schäffer, Letter of 18 February 1920, in: BKR Abt. C.A.S. Proc. sup. perqu. Scriptorum D. 77–130 K. 11 (quoted from the original).

A Poem of Illness and Operation

*1.
Still a child, so young in years
carefree and full of happiness
I did not yet know life's cares
My heart was filled with satisfaction.
2.
But soon it was quite otherwise
My Lord's hand grabbed me
Illness brought me pain and sorrow
And led me to a bitter sickbed.
3.
To lie down on the operating table
Took a lot of courage
And I did so thirty times
And there offered up my pain and blood.
4.
At those times I thought of my loved ones
And to everyone I said: Farewell!
Then a glance at the One who suffered on the cross
from whose wounds flows my salvation!
5.
I wanted always to give Him my love
And to die for Him too in this hour
Those were my last words
That's what I wished for with my heart and mouth!
6.
They gave me the chloroform
So disgustingly, sickeningly sweet
My every nerve became stronger
Until I lost consciousness.
7.
My extremities were as heavy as lead
Thunder resounded in my head
And I could no longer comprehend
What happened to me after that.
8.
And if I were to try to describe my awakening
I cannot even find the words*

Because no one can understand
Unless they have felt it for themselves.
9.
For a long time I lay there fantasizing
saying everything that was in my heart
the pain, oh, so burning
Brought me back to consciousness!
10.
A hard, bitter sickbed
Has chained me long and hard
so painful because of the many wounds
and yet so comforting and sublime!
11.
One thing has always remained with me –
An inner, peaceful trust in God
That in the difficult hours allows me
To rely always firmly on His help!
12.
My loved one lives on the holy Throne
That His grace always shows me
And each day He nourishes my sickly soul
In the Sacrament of Love
13.
And so I am not left here
in suffering and loneliness
I rejoice in those hours
that allow me to see: Eternity!
14.
Lord, bend down soon
And take me by the hand
And lead your sick little lamb
Into the land of peace!
15.
Now I am no longer lonely
In my quiet blessedness
I rest in Your Heart
Consecrated to You for eternity![106]

---

[106] Note of 12 August 1919, in: BKR Abt. C.A.S. Proc. sup. perqu. Scriptorum D. 44–76 K. 10 (quoted from the original).

Excerpts from Anna Schäffer's Letters

Cross and suffering

"Constantly on the cross to hang – with Jesus, my dear Redeemer: – That is my happiness! To love and to suffer and, when God wills it: That is my longing! – To die, O my Jesus, and see You, – what a happy lot awaits me: That is my hope!"[107]

"I would like to lay each little flower of suffering at the wounded heart of my heavenly Bridegroom, – so as to console and delight Him. Oh, that my love for you, o my Jesus, would give wings to my heart, so that I could fly to Your holy cross – to your most Sacred Heart – to the tabernacle, and before the throne of love I would like my heart to be assumed and consumed in yours. I know quite well that Your Heart is a deeply wounded heart – and therefore I, too, if I want to belong to Your heart, must be ready to live a life wounded in sacrifice – ready to bear the cross and suffering."[108]

"I have no other wish on earth than to be consumed in the fire of Your Most Sacred Heart, O my Jesus, and to help save a whole flock of souls for You, o my Saviour, so that you can draw all of them with Your grace into heaven."[109]

Eucharist

"The sun of my life is Jesus in the Most Blessed Sacrament ..!"[110]

"O Jesus, how happy the heart that loves you and always knows how to find you in the Holy Eucharist".[111]

"Oh, I would like to counsel all those who are suffering and all the souls who are in sorrow, to pour out their heart to the Blessed Sacrament and the star of love and consolation will enlighten their heart."[112]

"And until I am able to set off on the great mission, – to Jesus in heaven, I will in quiet and hiddenness bear my little cross of suffering and may it be a small sin-offering for the dear Saviour, for all the abuses heaped upon Him in the Most Blessed Sacrament. My God, I thank You, – My God, I love You!"[113]

---

[107] Note of 12 August 1919, in: BKR Abt. C.A.S. Proc. sup. perqu. Scriptorum D. 44–76 K. 10 (quoted from the original).
[108] Anna Schäffer, Letter of 1 September 1920, in: BKR Abt. C.A.S. Proc. sup. perqu. Scriptorum D. 77–130 K. 11 (quoted from the original).
[109] Anna Schäffer, Letter of 12 March 1921, in: BKR Abt. C.A.S. Proc. sup. perqu. Scriptorum D. 77–130 K. 11 (quoted from the original).
[110] Anna Schäffer, Letter of 28 December 1921, in: BKR Abt. C.A.S. Proc. sup. perqu. Scriptorum D. 77–130 K. 11 (quoted from the original).
[111] Anna Schäffer, Letter of 28 November 1922, in: BKR Abt. C.A.S. Proc. sup. perqu. Scriptorum D. 131–183 K. 12 quoted from the original).
[112] Anna Schäffer, Letter of 17 September 1917, in: BKR Abt. C.A.S. Acts 1915–1920 K. 18 quoted from the original).
[113] Anna Schäffer, Letter of 7 January 1920, in: BKR Abt. C.A.S. Proc. sup. perqu. Scriptorum D. 77–130 K. 11 (quoted from the original).

"[...] whenever I was really sick and, for example, was so sick all night long that I could not speak a word, as morning and time for Holy Communion approached (the suffering) was always a little lighter an hour before Communion, so that I could prepare myself and (this relief) also lasted an hour after Holy Communion, in such a way that I could make my little preparation and my Act of Thanksgiving. And this time it happened like that for several days and after that I got worse. Until this day I have never been happier to be able to receive Holy Communion than when I am really very sick." [114]

"[...] united with Jesus, every burden becomes light to bear – because in Holy Communion He gives us the strength we need." [115]

"Praised be Jesus in the Holy Eucharist [...] I can find neither words nor anything else to make myself understood; I would only like to say that in this instant I am bathed in an unspeakable bliss" [116].

---

114 Anna Schäffer, Letter of 24 December 1916, in: BKR Abt. C.A.S. Proc. sup. perqu. Scriptorum S. I–IV D. 1–43 K. 9 (quoted from the original).
115 Anna Schäffer, Letter of 18 November 1916, in: BKR Abt. C.A.S. Proc. sup. perqu. Scriptorum S. I–IV D. 1–43 K. 9 (quoted from the original).
116 Anna Schäffer, Drawing with extant date of 13 November 1918, in BKR Abt. C.A.S. Proc. sup. perqu. Scriptorum D. 44–76 K. 10 (quoted from the original).

Excerpts from Anna Schäffer's Thoughts And Memories Of My Life Of Illness And My Longing For The Eternal Homeland![117]

'Take up your cross and follow me!' These words from the Imitation of Christ with which the dear Saviour invites me to follow Him are the foundation stone of my heart in which the cross is set. With love and gratitude I will greet each moment – and in love of the cross and gratitude for the cross shall I draw my last life's breath!

'On the cross - and in Holy Communion, O my Lord and God, have I learned to love you!'

O my God I want to lovingly accept the cross that You offer me. How could I struggle against it? No, my Jesus, I promised You when I dedicated myself as an offering for souls, that I want to accept from Your hand every cross that You see fit to send me. Shall I not also rejoice when day after day you place a cross upon my shoulders and thereby give me an opportunity to make reparation to Your divine Heart for sins? O my Jesus, I want to embrace this little cross lovingly and unto my last breath may it be my joy, my glory and my delight. I want to be totally dead to the world and not glory in anything except the cross of Jesus, my divine Bridegroom, through Whom the world is crucified to me and I to the world. I long for no treasure other than holy poverty, no other delight than His suffering, no other love than He Himself. It matters not to me what others do, think or say, - in truth I am only what I am in God's eyes. We can never think too humbly of ourselves; we must come to the point that in the eyes of others we are quite imperfect, rather than give in to our self-love whenever an opportunity for self-humiliation presents itself. O my God, You alone know how poor, wretched and imperfect I am in Your holy eyes; be gracious and merciful to me, a poor sinner.

---

[117] The original of Anna Schäffers „Gedanken und Erinnerungen meines Krankenlebens – and meine Sehnsucht nach der ewigen Heimat!" (Thoughts And Memories Of My Life Of Illness And My Longing For The Eternal Homeland) is found in: BKR Abt. CAS K. 12a XII.; published in: Schwager Georg Franz X. (ed.), Thoughts and Memories of my Life of Illness and my Longing for the Eternal Homeland, Verlag Schnell & Steiner GmbH, Regensburg 2012.

Significant Dates in the Life of Anna Schäffer

1882 (18 February)   Birth and Baptism in Mindelstetten
1888-1895   School years
1893 (12 April)   First Holy Communion in Mindelstetten
1894 (16 July)   Confirmation in Neustadt an der Donau
1895   Began working in order to earn a dowry needed to enter religious life
1896 (25 January)   Death of her father
1898 (June)   Informed of her suffering in a dream in Landshut
1901 (4 February)   Tragic accident in Stammham when she fell into boiling lye
1910 (4 October)   Dream with ensuing mystical stigmatisation
1925 (5 October)   Death in Mindelstetten
1925 (8 October)   Burial by Father Carl Rieger in the parish cemetery in Mindelstetten
1972 (26 July)   Translation of her remains to the Parish Church in Mindelstetten
1973 (17 March)   Opening of the Process of Beatification by Bishop Rudolf Graber of Regensburg
1995 (11 July)   Recognition of her heroic virtues by Pope John Paul II
1999 (7 March)   Beatification in St. Peter's Basilica in Rome by Pope John Paul II
2012 (21 October)   Canonisation by Pope Benedict XVI in Rome

Bibliography / References:

Andrea Ambrosi, Informatio super virtutibus, in: Congregatio de Causis Sanctorum P. N. 1354 – Ratisbonensis Canonizationis Servae Dei Annae Schäffer iuvenis saecularis (1882–1925) Positio super virtutibus, Roma 1992.

The Bible.

Die Feier des Stundengebetes. Eigenfeiern des Bistums Regensburg. Authentische Ausgabe for den liturgischen Gebrauch. Herausgegeben im Auftrag des Bischofs von Regensburg, Regensburg 2011.

Die Tagespost, 19 January2012/Nr. 8.

"Im Leiden habe ich Dich lieben gelernt!". Die Schriften Anna Schäffers. Dokumentiert von Emmeram H. Ritter, Regensburg 1999.

Ritter Emmeram H., Anna Schäffer. Eine Selige aus Bayern, Regensburg 2012.

Schwager Georg Franz X. (ed.), Thoughts and Memories of my Life of Illness and my Longing for the Eternal Homeland, Verlag Schnell & Steiner GmbH, Regensburg 2012.

Schwager Georg Franz X. (ed.), Liebe wächst im Leiden. Die selige Anna Schäffer von Mindelstetten. Kurzbiographie-Novene/Gebete -Gedanken, Regensburg, 4th edition, 2006.

Schwaiger Georg, Anna Schäffer von Mindelstetten. Ein Leben in der Gnade Gottes, Regensburg, 4th edition, 2000.

Selige Anna Schäffer von Mindelstetten/Bayern July 1999, Letter 35, published by the Department for Causes of Beatification and Canonisation of the Episcopal Consistory of the Diocese of Regensburg 1999.

Selige Anna Schäffer von Mindelstetten/Bayern December 1999, Letter 36, published by the Department for Causes of Beatification and Canonisation of the Episcopal Consistory of the Diocese of Regensburg 1999.

Selige Anna Schäffer von Mindelstetten/Bayern December 2000, Letter 38, published by the Department for Causes of Beatification and Canonisation of the Episcopal Consistory of the Diocese of Regensburg 2000.

Selige Anna Schäffer von Mindelstetten/Bayern December 2009, Letter 56 published by the Department for Causes of Beatification and Canonisation of the Episcopal Consistory of the Diocese of Regensburg 2009.

Selige Anna Schäffer von Mindelstetten/Bayern December 2010, Letter 58, published by the Department for Causes of Beatification and Canonisation of the Episcopal Consistory of the Diocese of Regensburg 2010.

Selige Anna Schäffer von Mindelstetten/Bayern December 2011, Letter 60, published by the Department for Causes of Beatification and Canonisation of the Episcopal Consistory of the Diocese of Regensburg 2011.

Stärke Deine Brüder. Homilies, Addresses and Conferences of Bishop Rudolf Graber. Published by the Cathedral Chapter of the Diocese of Regensburg on the occasion of the Diocesan Ordinary's 75th birthday, Regensburg 1978.

Weigl Alfons Maria, Geschichte einer Liebe, Altötting, 15th edition 1998.

Remarks at the graveside of the virgin Anna Schäfer (sic!), who suffered and sacrificed for 25 years in Mindelstetten. Given on 8 October 1925 by Rev. Father Karl Rieger. Habbel Brothers' Press, Regensburg, o.J.

Abbreviations:

Abt.	Department for Beatification and Canonisation Processes
Anm.	Note
AS	Anna Schäffer
BKR	Diocesan Curia, Regensburg
C.A.S.	Cause for the Beatification/Canonisation of Anna Schäffer
D.	Document
K.	Carton
Nr.	Number
o. J.	Year not indicated
Proc.	process
sup.	super
perqu.	perquisitio

Manuscripts mentioned in the text can be found in:

BKR Abt. C.A.S. Proc. sup. perqu. Scriptorum S. I–IV D. 1–43 K. 9.

BKR Abt. C.A.S. Proc. sup. perqu. Scriptorum D. 44–76 K. 10.

BKR Abt. C.A.S. Proc. sup. perqu. Scriptorum D. 77–130 K. 11.

BKR Abt. C.A.S. Proc. sup. perqu. Scriptorum D. 131–183 K. 12.

BKR Abt. C.A.S. Proc. sup. perqu. Scriptorum D. I–XIII K. 12a.

BKR Abt. C.A.S. Transcriptions: Thoughts and Memories/ Dream book/ Poetry/ Accounts concerning AS K. 16.

BKR Abt. C.A.S. Acts 1915–1920 K. 18.

BKR Abt. C.A.S. Acts 1926–1930 K. 20.

Description of the portrait of Anna Schäffer, oil painting by Winifried Tonner, 1999 (on page 34):

The image shows Anna Schäffer in her God-given life's task, understanding her illness as a gift of divine love offered in union with the suffering of Jesus Christ. Over her head is the Sacred Heart of Jesus, which she so greatly revered. The depiction of the Heart of Jesus is an original drawing from Anna's letters. It is recognizable iconographically with the flames shooting from the Heart. Here, however, we do not have the usual depiction of the flames of fire, but of ears of wheat. This is an unmistakable reference to the Sacrament of the Holy Eucharist. From Holy Communion Anna Schäffer drew the strength to accept her cross, her suffering and pain. Then too we find in the painting the main points of her apostolate: prayer, symbolized by the rosary; her letter-writing apostolate in the form of the letters placed in front of her and an indication of her handiwork in the embroidered cloth above her head. Anna Schäffer's life and suffering lay in the shadow, but also in the sign, of the cross. The artist, Winifried Tonner († 2002) indicated this by constructing the composition of the painting with the horizontal and vertical, with Anna Schäffer's head placed at the point the two planes intersect. The above-mentioned embroidered cloth serves as the "titulus" of the cross.